Graduate
Savvy

Graduate
Savvy

Navigating the World of Online Higher Education

2nd Edition

Jeffrey L. Green, Ph.D.

Glocal Press
Warrenton, Virginia 20187

Editing: Pamela K. S. Patrick, Ph.D.

Cover Image: Fotolia

Printed in the United States of America.

ISBN: 978-0-9817116-1-4

Published by:
Glocal Press
Warrenton, Virginia 20187
www.glocalpress.com

Library of Congress Control Number: 2010926087

To my wonderful wife, Kathy,
and two incredible children, Justin and Alexandra.

I have said a million times and will a million more —
I am the luckiest husband and father on the entire planet.

The winds and waves
are always on the side
of the ablest navigators.

~*Edward Gibbon*
1737 - 1794

Contents

Foreword

We live in interesting times in the world of higher education. Access to graduate education has expanded exponentially with the advent of the Internet, creating opportunities to pursue advanced degrees that previously could not be imagined. With the availability of degree programs offered through online delivery systems, adults who have "day jobs" can now attend classes offered in asynchronous learning environments that optimize flexible use of time while offering the convenience of anytime, any place course participation. Figuring out how this different paradigm of learning will "fit" the needs of prospective students, as well as how to embark on a journey of graduate education, is the focus of Jeff Green's insightful, focused, and highly practical text.

By titling his book *Graduate Savvy*, Dr. Green underscores the need to know and understand what graduate online education is all about. "Savvy" refers to being able to grasp or understand, and when applied to online graduate school, highlights a perspective that is especially appealing to adults who are returning to the education arena. Through the well crafted sequence of book sections and chapters, the text provides guidance and hands-on advice about how to successfully engage with the graduate education process. At each step along the degree completion pathway, readers will become savvy in the ways of online learning from prepping for each upcoming class to writing in an academic voice to moving through the capstone stage of the doctoral program: The comprehensive examination and the dissertation.

Dr. Green's personal experiences of being a highly qualified professional, a graduate of an online doctoral program and an online adjunct faculty member supports the wisdom he shares about his personal graduate savvy. He's gone through each of the steps he outlines in the book and uses this knowledge to inform each chapter. He speaks to the reader through a conversation that inspires and motivates, yet also makes it clear that seeking a doctoral degree will require fortitude, focus, and a fire in the belly. These qualities will determine how each person approaches the challenge of completing a graduate program as each critical next step nears.

The strengths of this text, making it relevant and immediately valuable to the reader, are found throughout each chapter. Practical information that can be immediately evaluated and applied is characteristic of each element in the text. Keeping it next to the reader's study space will ensure that it becomes a ready reference and source of continuing inspiration. Adults who are balancing real world responsibilities of job, family, and the complexities of life will find that having access to the insights accrued by a professional who has personal knowledge of each stage of the educational process will be a source of affirmation and motivation.

Pam Patrick, PhD
Academic Director of Colloquia Capella University

Preface

We shall not cease from exploration,
and the end of all our exploring
will be to arrive where we started
and know the place for the first time.

~T. S. Elliot

Lighting the Fire

What a great time to be a student or teacher in higher education! Innovations in teaching pedagogies, expanding understandings of how adults really do learn, and the exponential growth of the Internet form the perfect storm for one of our most endearing values: Opportunity! Never has there been a greater opportunity to learn and teach than today. Online learning, quite literally, is transforming the world of higher education.

> *Education is not the filling of a pail,*
> *but the lighting of a fire.*
>
> *~William Butler Yeats*

The ultimate purpose of education should be to expand the way we actually see the world...to enhance our critical thinking skills to enable us to get beyond what is known and see the *potential*. Sure, teachers need to pass on rote information, but real education explodes like fireworks when students actually begin to see what they have always seen but in new and exciting ways. As T. S. Elliot so eloquently voiced, even if we have seen or experienced something many times, the real challenge is to see it differently, from a new perspective, each and every time.

Providing Insights and Navigation

The intent of this text is not necessarily to share new revelations about the future of education. It simply is to help wrap your mind around the world of online learning and help you succeed should you decide to enroll in a web-based program. Through observations, humble insights, and insider experiences, I hope this informal and relaxed text will help readers gain a better understanding of the powerful paradigm shift in higher education that we are now experiencing.

These insights are offered with the greatest humility. Socrates observed, "Although I do not suppose that either of us knows anything really beautiful and good, I am better off than he is – for he knows nothing, and thinks that he knows. I neither know nor think that I know. In this matter particular, then, I seem to have slightly the advantage of him." I have devoted years to learning, teaching, researching, and developing courses in both traditional and online universities. Yet clearly, I do not have all the answers. Indeed, much of this book was written based on countless interviews and conversations with tremendous input from students, faculty, and many others literally around the world. Two chapters were authored by colleagues who have a tremendous expertise in the areas of beginning an online program and the dissertation process. Dr. Ben Noah authored Chapter 7 *FirstCourse,* and Dr. Curtis Brant authored Chapter 19 *Dissertation Strategies for Success.* Dr. Julia Moore offered specific insights on Chapter 16 *Comprehensive Exam Strategies for Success.* Dr. Pamela Patrick provided tremendous wisdom regarding nearly every aspect of the book.

My paradigms of higher education have been shaped by many influences not the least of which are my experiences with Virginia Commonwealth University, the University of Virginia, Capella University, and the FBI Academy. Of course, my insights do not necessarily reflect the views of these institutions of higher learning.

What's New with the 2nd Edition

The first edition was received with much greater enthusiasm and appreciation than we ever imagined. And with such a wide readership came great ideas and suggestions for the next edition. Let me briefly mention some of the bigger changes.

The opening chapters have been updated to provide a current picture of where online education sits today with regard to value and respect. Included are comments on online higher education from Minnesota Governor Tim Pawlenty, CNN Political Analyst and Presidential Advisor David Gergen, and former Secretary of State General Colin Powel. Substantive changes also have been made in the navigation chapters. For example, the chapter on academic writing has been completely revamped to encompass the newest APA Publication Manual (APA 6th edition). The chapters on scholarly sources and plagiarism have been expanded. The chapters concerning the doctoral comprehensive exam have been enhanced with sample comments from graders. The bottom line is that we kept the heart and soul of the first edition but gave the concepts a fresh look, offered new perspectives, and discussed the latest trends and best practices available.

The Audience

As with most authors, I hope the book finds interested readers in a variety of places. We certainly saw this with the publication of the first edition. One of the most valuable goals of the book is to offer specific and demonstrable strategies to successfully navigate and complete a higher education degree. Topics such as effectively navigating the course room, colloquium, comprehensive exam, and dissertation are highlights that make this a must read for learners at any stage of their journey.

I trust my faculty colleagues also will enjoy the text as a method of sharing best practices and building a stronger sense of community among learners and faculty. In this context, the book serves as a tool to enhance open discourse between learners and faculty. Honest dialogue is a powerful learning tool. As instructors may agree or differ with a particular point in the book or know a better practice, they can share these sentiments with learners thus opening a valuable dialogue that otherwise may not have occurred. This allows the book to serve as an awareness tool and furthers student/faculty engagement.

The value of the text also well extends beyond online education. I interact with traditional and online universities throughout the world on a daily basis. I assure you, while not all of the insights in this book apply beyond the online setting, the vast majority of them will have direct relevance to any endeavor in higher education.

Lastly, I hope *Graduate Savvy* will offer the curious and uninformed an objective overview and fresh perspective concerning the tremendous impact of online learning. It is my sincere intention to offer a realistic sense of the value of online education and a strong feel for how it all works.

Jeff Green

Acknowledgments

Plain and simple, it takes a lot of hard work and effort from many different people to write a book. Sometimes that diligence comes long before the book was ever a glimmer in the author's eyes. Thanks Mom and Dad for all you have done over the years. In your different ways, you taught me that children can become anything and anyone they want to be. You showed me what perseverance and risk-taking really look like. Most importantly, you have always been in my corner when I needed you most. What a great legacy.

I also want to give a huge thanks to my wife and children. This book truly was a family effort - numerous Saturday nights at Borders and Barnes and Noble, countless dinner conversations about what to include or take out, mutual teaching and learning about specific topics such as plagiarism and scholarly writing, even the design of the book cover. Thank you Kathy, Justin, and Alexandra for all of your guidance, enthusiasm, and unyielding support.

I have learned so much over the years from so many great teachers and mentors that it would be impossible to name them all. Yet, I have to name a few who directly influenced my ability to write this book. A big thank you to Dr. Charles Tiffin, Dr. Alice Yick-Flanagan, and Dr. John Sullivan. A special thanks as well to Mr. Mike Vezo for mentoring me in the wonderful world of publishing.

I also wish to thank Dr. Ben Noah for his contribution in writing Chapter 7 and Dr. Curtis Brant for his contribution in writing Chapter 19. I also would like to thank Dr. Julia Moore for offering her expertise in Chapter 16 and for serving as the primary content reviewer for the text. Lastly, thank you to Dr. Pamela Patrick for her insights, enthusiasm, and can do spirit and for taking the time to write the foreword and offering her keen wisdom with regard to nearly every aspect of the book. It is these contributions that took *Graduate Savvy* from a B to an A.

Chapter 21 would not have been possible without a few friends and colleagues who offered to share their personal distance learning experiences. Thank you to Dr. Rodney Hick, Dr. Greg Vecchi, Ms. Amy Williamson, Dr. Benjamin Davis, and Dr. Charles Tiffin.

Finally, I would like to thank Dr. Debbie Beebe, Mr. Charles Taylor, Dr. Kathy Mitchell, and Mr. Charles Robb, Jr. for taking the time to read the manuscript and offering such wonderful endorsements for the cover.

Part
I

The New Paradigm in Higher Education

Creating Access to Education

The beginning of knowledge is the discovery of something we do not understand.

~*Frank Herbert*

Online higher education probably represents the single greatest paradigm shift in higher education since the advent of the university. Yet, many people do not understand this phenomenon. Occasionally, I still get looks of puzzlement or disbelief when asked about the value of online learning. Yet, a little bafflement among the populace is not necessarily a bad thing. As Kahlil Gibran observed, "Perplexity is the beginning of knowledge."

Universities are increasingly becoming more competitive in order to stay relevant in an ever changing educational market. As traditional, brick and mortar schools embrace distance learning initiatives and online universities continue to exceed high standards, our society is becoming more familiar and accepting of online degrees. According to the Distance Education and Training Council (DETC), online enrollment presently is rising at an astonishing 33 percent a year. More than 80 percent of students today have taken an online course, and this number is expected to climb to almost 100 percent in just a few years (Babb & Mirabella, 2007). Almost 20 percent of all U.S. higher education students took at least one online course in the fall of 2006. This represents 3.5 million students, which was a 10 percent increase over the number reported in 2005. This double digit growth rate for online enrollments far surpasses the 1.5 percent growth of the overall higher education student populace (Sloan Consortium, 2007). In almost all educational venues, a "shift in organizational structure and pedagogy [has occurred] to accommodate distance teaching and learning" (Clark & Ramsey, p. 397).

Web-based higher education is not coming; it is upon us and has already redefined the world of higher education. Part I speaks to this very issue by exploring the idea of online higher education and the multitude of benefits and value associated with earning your degree through the web. Enjoy!

Anybody who understands the generation that is behind us knows they live a big chunk of their life online. Anyone who resists the notion that the future is not online or a big part of it is online is not in my view thinking comprehensively, holistically, or in a forward-leaning way. The future is not about sometimes gifted, sometimes not gifted, lecturers standing at whiteboards droning on as assistant professors to mass numbers of students in Econ 101.

The generation that is coming up behind learns, consumes, and shares information in a fundamentally different way. That leans right into online learning. The future is clear in that regard. The only question is who is going to lead it and who is going to follow.

*~Governor Tim Pawlenty
Minnesota*

Chapter

1

Exploring the Idea of Web-based Higher Education

The principal goal of education is to create men who are capable of doing new things, not simply of repeating what other generations have done.

~Jean Piaget

Can I Really Learn in an Online Environment?

The answer is an unequivocal yes! I have talked with people across the world about their experiences in higher education. I am particularly fascinated by their perceptions and personal paradigms. Of course, opinions and insights run the gamut, but one perception appears to flow constant when I speak to people who have experienced traditional and web-based higher education. They almost always feel they received an outstanding education in their online endeavors. In fact, in the 2008 Annual Reports from all Distance Education and Training Council (DETC) universities, 95% of the learners felt they had reached their goal, 96% were satisfied with their education, and 95% said they would recommend their studies to a friend.

> *For me, online education is much more demanding with regard to timelines, readings, and even rigor. These higher expectations actually create a stronger learning environment than in many traditional, face-to-face classrooms.*
>
> *~Stephen Smith*
> *Ph.D. learner*
> *Northcentral University*
> *Class of 2009*

People are different and have differing learning preferences. We all digest information in our unique way. Some prefer dynamic and charismatic instructors while others would much rather have a mild-mannered professor who just presents the facts. Some students like discussing abstract ideas, while others prefer hands on demonstrations. Some prefer to work in groups, and others would rather work alone. Some folks are hard-chargers, and some are procrastinators. But these are just preferences. If humans are anything, we are flexible and adaptable. Indeed, the greatest leaders in history were the ones who responded to the needs of their followers and the demands of the situation regardless if the intervention was within their comfort zone or not. We all have our own individual style of learning, and we all can learn effectively regardless of the platform!

A consistent theme in the literature is that distance education models are, at minimum, just as effective as traditional models of delivery (Moulton & Moulton, 2006). However, there is an expanding body of research indicating some students actually may learn better in a web-based program. Gilbert (2001) reported a study in which an identical graduate course was taught simultaneously at three different schools. The first two universities, Georgia Tech and the University of Alabama, offered the course in a traditional, face-to-face format. The third university, National Technical University, offered the course in an online format. The result was that online students learned more and developed a stronger sense of community than their counterparts in the brick and mortar courses.

Gubernick & Ebeling (1997) noted a research project by the University of Phoenix that determined exam grades of its web-based students were 5% to 10% higher than students of competing brick and mortar programs in three other Arizona universities. Similarly, Vasarhelyi and Graham (1997) found in their research at the University of Michigan that web-based delivery produced higher average grades than traditional platforms.

Meyer (2006) conducted a study of students taking a graduate-level course on Historical and Policy Perspectives in Higher Education. The course was delivered in both a face-to-face and online discussion format. Upon completion of each topic area within the course, the students were asked to assess various feelings in an effort to compare their face-to-face and online experiences. The results of the study indicated students were more uncomfortable in the face-to-face discussions on political tolerance, affirmative action, and gender. They were more concerned about their classmates' feelings in the face-to-face discussions on diversity and political tolerance. They were more likely to share a commonality with classmates in the online discussions of political tolerance, affirmative action, and gender. Lastly, the students were more disposed to engage in discourse with classmates in the online environment concerning the topics of diversity and academic freedom. Online discussions actually created a greater sense of community than face-to-face discussions.

Gallagher (2005) and her associates at the University of Pennsylvania compared educational outcomes from a dental hygiene course offered online and in a traditional classroom. As with Meyer's research, the results were intriguing. Learners in the web-based course demonstrated significantly higher motivation and learning success based on grades and completion of assignments and projects. Most importantly, knowledge retention of the class material, as measured six months after completion of the course, was greater with students who completed the course in the online setting.

In the DETC's 2009 annual report, they reported the findings of a Department of Education meta-study of 51 research reports (ones that met a rigorous research design criteria) conducted since 1996. They found that students who took all or part of their instruction online *performed better* than those taking the same course through face-to-face instruction.

The literature is fairly consistent with regard to adult learning. The method of delivery is seldom the predominant factor in learning efficacy. The most significant influences toward true learning are the design of the course, teaching style, academic rigor, a strong sense of community, and the individual motivation and drive the student brings to the course.

Why Do Many Students Learn Better in the Online Classroom?

Web-based learning is much easier, much faster, and negates the need for interaction with your classmates. Right? Well, not quite… in fact, not in the slightest! Online learning is more difficult in many ways and actually requires heightened engagement in the classroom. If the learning platform, be it web-based or face-to-face, is not the determinant factor of student effectiveness, then why do many students appear to do better in the online environment?

For starters, there is no hiding in the back of the class. Everyone in an online setting participates. Remember those occasions back in your undergrad days when you did not complete the assigned readings. What happened when the professor raised a question to the class? You probably crouched down a little and let your more eager classmates raise their hands. You probably were successful by simply letting your peers carry the day. This does not occur in the online environment. In many web-based programs, discussion questions are posted in the beginning of the week, and every student must respond to the question. Additionally, each learner is required to respond to a specified minimal number of peer postings. In other words, substantive class participation in the weekly discussions is not only encouraged; it is mandated. In fact, the discussion postings are actually graded in many online programs with regard to substance, writing skills, critical thinking, and even appropriate citations and references.

This high level of accountability found in the online learning environment may account in some measure for the high value students place on this type of education. A myth in higher education is that instructors who give students less work, fewer challenges, a slower pace, and higher grades are rewarded with higher evaluations. In Young's (2006) research concerning learner perspectives of web-based instruction in higher education, she determined that students thought the most valuable classes were the ones in which professors set a high bar with lofty but achievable goals. Similarly, Marsh (2001) found that instructors who assigned greater amounts of work and had very high expectations were the ones that learners viewed as the most effective.

Certainly, there are other elements of effective learning beyond accountability. Young and Shaw (1999) determined, in their research of teacher efficacy, the best learning atmosphere consisted of effective communication among students and the teacher, a relaxed learning environment, teacher concern for students, and effective organization of the classroom. Clearly, these elements can be found just as readily in a web-based course as in a traditional classroom.

Final Thoughts

The bottom line is that some people will always prefer the face-to-face learning environment. That's okay. Diversity, in any context, makes us stronger. Yet, I ask you not to make prejudgments about online learning until you have tried it. I can't tell you how many friends and colleagues have told me that they would not do well in an online program because they need face-to-face interaction. Yet, after experiencing an online course, their entire view changed.

Do not allow yourself to fall into the most common trap in humanity: *Status Quo*. Where would we be without Einstein's imagination and will to explore beyond what was accepted? What would the world look like without Walt Disney's unbridled vision and perseverance? How different would our global paradigms be without Gandhi's soft spoken but powerful intellect and ability to think beyond the known? Where would our country be without the power, conviction, and *dream* of Dr. Martin Luther King, Jr.?

> *What you learners are doing are getting real time education in the most powerful way with the most powerful tools and with a great faculty that watches you go through all of this. This is the future of education.*
>
> *General Colin Powell, USA (Ret.)*
> *In an address to online Ph.D. learners at Capella University's October 2009 Colloquium*

We are all different and have different learning preferences and styles. In fact, my personal preference is a blended approach incorporating face-to-face and online approaches. I sincerely believe most adult learners will value the extremely personal and interactive educational experience, flexibility, and increased access to higher education that web-based learning offers. The majority of learners will recognize that an online education may offer enhanced communication and socialization in a distinctive and wonderful platform.

Chapter

2

> # Why
> # Choose
> # Online
> # Learning?

Why is online learning emerging at such an extraordinary rate? While there are many attractions of online learning, possibly the greatest explanation of its growth rests with the change in us. Children today experience web-based learning before even entering elementary school. As this generation stretches from pre-school to early adulthood, their familiarity and comfort with computer based learning alleviates the hang-ups and skepticism that many older adults may have about online learning. Indeed, this contemporary generation of learners entering post secondary education actually expects their programs and teachers to incorporate technology into the learning environment.

The second component of this phenomenon is the heightened interest in advanced education among working adults. Our thirst for life-long learning actually intensifies as we grow older. You probably have experienced this yourself or seen it in others. Many adults decided in their youth not to pursue formal education or were unable to because of a variety of reasons. Or they may have earned their bachelor's degree after high school but never figured out how to continue their formal education once the

> *Working couples, single parents, and independent workers of all ages and diverse living situations benefit from these programs and services, which promote work-life balance and enable the pursuit of a higher education.*
>
> *University of Phoenix*

demands of life crept in. As life moved on, family, work, and the daily routines of living seemed to push higher education further and further away. Sure, money may have been a factor years ago and still may be, but the real obstacle was the lack of convenient and realistic access to college.

Today, working adults (young and old) are going back to school in record numbers. In fact, according to the Distance Education and Training Council (DETC), 90 percent of distance learners attending degree programs accredited by the DETC work full time. Online higher education largely is responsible for this vast new wave of adult learners.

Increased Access to Higher Education

Unquestionably, web-based learning provides alternative opportunities to potential students who otherwise would not have access to post secondary education. Geographical barriers are removed thus expanding access to formal education to anyone, anywhere. Students no longer have to move to the city or to campus towns to earn their degrees. They no longer have to commute long distances to get to class. They can attend college from their homes in rural areas, suburbs, mountains, or by the ocean. As long as you have access to the Internet, you have access to an outstanding college education.

A subcomponent of this expanded access is the opportunity for students to earn a degree in a field specific to their wants and needs. I know so many people who earned degrees in fields that really did not interest them and were a far stretch from their work requirements simply because the local university did not offer the program they needed. A good friend even earned a Doctorate of Education (Ed.D.) instead of the Ph.D. in criminal justice that he really wanted because there was no local access to such a program.

The indirect benefit presented by additional educational programs offered by online universities is similar to the same value presented by a free economic market. As web-based specializations and degrees expand, traditional brick and mortar schools have begun to expand their offerings. It's competition 101. Brick and mortar schools will not be able to keep up with online offerings because of limited students in their geographical areas, but competition has forced them to broaden their degrees and specializations beyond traditional means.

> *Online education is about creating agile learners who can operate in both human and technological environments with equal comfort. In my view, the greatest contribution of online education may not be conquering time and distance, but educating people for a new century.*
>
> *~Dr. Gerald A. Heeger*
> *President*
> *University of Maryland*
> *University College*

15

The idea of distance learning never entered my mind when I initially was looking at doctoral programs. I had attended traditional brick and mortar schools for my undergraduate and master's degree. It wasn't that I was afraid of web-based learning; it just never entered my learning paradigm. After the events of September 11, 2001, and after a transfer to the Washington DC area, I found myself in a world of uncertainty about seeking the Ph.D. With the opportunity (or threat – depending on your outlook) of being transferred several times throughout my career, I realistically did not know if I would be in one place long enough to complete a doctoral program. It was then that I started looking into web-based higher education. I can tell you now, with several years of hindsight, that I could not have completed my Ph.D. in a traditional university. Just the additional demands on my time with regard to commuting would have presented a significant barrier. Most importantly, the flexibility that online higher education offered me was the opportunity to complete the program even if I had to move from one part of the world to the other.

Convenience and Flexibility

Learners in Northrup's (2002) research indicated that flexibility was one of the most significant reasons they chose web-based higher education. Web-based learning offers unique convenience to learners whose daily responsibilities will not allow them to attend classes at fixed times. Learners also often comment that the opportunity to attend classes on their schedule allows them to engage classmates with more preparation and relevance. Some schools still prefer to use *synchronous* platforms in which students actually meet at specified times to simulate a face-to-face classroom. My experience has been that this is the exception rather than the rule. Most online universities and online programs from brick and mortar schools use *asynchronous* learning platforms. In other words, there is no real time chatting. Discussions are answered in a threaded context enabling true flexibility for learners and the instructor. When I was a student, my favorite time to log-in was around 10:00 pm after everyone was in bed. I didn't get a lot of sleep for a few years, but graduate school is not designed to be easy. At least I could attend college on my time according to the demands of my schedule that particular day. Try finding a class at the local university from 10:00 pm to 1:00 am where you can wear your pajamas.

Another consideration is the time spent commuting to and from class. Early in my doctoral program, I was talking with a friend who was working on his doctorate at a traditional university. He was amazed at how much research and work I was required to put into the courses. His program was tough, but by his own admission, not like mine. This conversation led me to shamelessly go down a pity path and start complaining about all the hours each week just for one class. While he understood my woes, he had woes of his own. He looked at me with incredulous eyes and said, "Jeff, are you kidding me...I spend a minimum of three hours on the road each class just fighting I-95 traffic. Then there's parking, walking to class...I don't want to hear it." He was so right. I was putting in significant hours, but it could have been much worse.

Time is not the only issue. Consider the money that commuting costs. My wife paid upwards of $10.00 a day to park at George Mason University where she earned her Master's. This does not begin to account for the gas each way, the upkeep and additional mileage on the car, and most importantly, the time away from living her life that she instead had to spend sitting on I-66. How do you even put a price on that?

Online learning also offers convenience and flexibility to persons that would have physical difficulties attending a brick and mortar school. A web-based education removes or mitigates obstacles for persons with disabilities or older learners for whom driving and mobility issues present significant challenges.

Another convenience of web-based learning is that it offers the potential to complete your degree faster. Realistically, most learners take just as long in the web-based environment, but if you are a hard-charger, many programs do offer accelerated courses. Accelerated classes require you to do just as much work but in half or three fourths the time of a regular course. Yet, the most realistic reason why you can graduate faster is that most online programs allow you to take classes all year long. Instead of the traditional summer and fall semester with a possible summer semester in the middle, web-based programs generally consist of four semesters or quarters: Winter, spring, summer, and fall. So, you work harder with no breaks, but you also have the ability to graduate quicker. It's your choice!

Timely Feedback

Most working adults who take classes in traditional environments attend in the evenings or weekends. There simply are not many Monday/Wednesday/Friday or Tuesday/Thursday classes offered in the evenings, so most adult learners attend once a week classes usually for 2 ½ to 3 hours. At best, when you submit a paper Tuesday night, it will be the following Tuesday night before you get it back. This, generally, is not the case in the online environment. Time and space barriers do not exist in the web-based world of academe. Sure, it still may take an instructor a week to get a paper graded, particularly if he has 15 or 20 thirty page papers submitted at the same time or if the instructor is adjunct and has a full time career outside of the university. Yet, it is not unusual for online instructors to have your postings, assignments, or papers graded in just a few days. Even more important than the grades are the feedback and comments. Who wants to wait a week to get sound, constructive feedback that they could apply to other assignments or other courses?

This brings up another tremendous quality of online learning: the *iterative process*. Many online professors and universities have adopted an iterative process of learning. Some in the field of adult education refer to this concept as *Mastery of Learning*. Simply stated, this process means give and take towards self-development and improvement. For example, in my face-to-face and online courses, it is not uncommon for me to return papers without a grade. If the paper or assignment is an A, I simply make my comments throughout the paper regarding content and writing and then return it to the learner with the A. Yet, if the learner has submitted the paper early enough, and the paper is something less than an A, I often will return it with my comments but no grade. The learner has the choice of re-submitting it without changes or reworking the paper based on my comments. Only once in years of practicing the iterative process have I had a learner tell me to just grade it the way it was initially submitted! Learners want to learn. They want to do well and not just with regard to a grade. They want validation from their instructor that their hard work is paying off. Any professor in any university can practice the iterative process, but online learning is uniquely structured for this teaching paradigm. Just think about it. In the one week that the brick and mortar student had to wait for his paper, the online student could have had several conversations and multiple revisions to his paper.

Ken Blanchard observed, "Feedback is the breakfast of champions." He made his remarks in the context of the leader-follower relationship, but the statement is just as true in any endeavor, particularly that of higher education. Online learning provides an exceptional platform for this critical component of learning and personal growth.

The Power of Diversity

Along with the enhanced capacity to break down geographical borders, web-based higher education offers a unique ability to bring together an incredibly diverse class with regard to values, cultures, gender, age, and all sorts of dynamic demographics. Diversity expands our capacity to bring new and stimulating ideas to the table, to expose students to different cultures, and ultimately affect the way learners see the world. It also brings a variety of resources to the class that you would not otherwise have access.

> *The most important help a professor can provide is honest, specific, and constructive feedback – and the quicker the better.*
>
> ~*Wade Ammerman*
> *Ph.D. learner*
> *Northcentral University*
> *Class of 2010*

I will never forget the two themes that former FBI Director Louis Freeh mentioned in nearly all of his speeches, presentations, and even informal gatherings. The first was that ethics must be the foundation for everything we do. The second theme was diversity. He continuously preached that the FBI's strength was its diversity. He was right, and higher education is no different!

A Strong Sense of Community

The human desire for belonging, a feeling of community, is one of our strongest and most fundamental needs. As Stephen Covey observed, "Next to physical survival, the greatest need of a human being is psychological survival – to be understood, to be affirmed, to be validated, to be appreciated." The essential elements of community appear to be dependence and reciprocity...a feeling of belonging, trust, shared perspectives, familiar values, mutual aspirations, validation, and common experiences among members (Anderson & Carter, 1999; Rohai, 2002). A deep sense of community plays a particularly important role in higher education.

Wehlage, Rutter, and Smith (1989) determined in their research that universities that paid particular attention to developing a sense of belonging, attachment, and involvement had significantly higher student retention rates. Tinto (1993) theorized that learners who have a strong sense of community with other students have increased levels of satisfaction with their program, which leads to greater student perseverance and success.

My assumption is that all colleges take the idea of community serious. Yet, because they have physical contact with their students, many traditional institutions may take for granted the nuances and responsibilities associated with building a strong community, particularly in the classroom. This is not the case with online universities and programs.

Online learners have tremendous opportunities to meet other professionals in their field and establish positive relationships. The vast majority of web-based courses see students conversing about theories and real life applicability way beyond the minimum posting requirements. The very nature of online learning requires extensive communication among students and faculty. This open and engaging communications infrastructure lends itself to strong community building.

Expanded Capacity to Build New Partnerships in a Global Society

In his 1987 autobiography, *Man of the House*, Tip O'Neill, former Speaker of the United States House of Representatives, shared a conversation he had with his father regarding Tip's election loss in his effort to become a Cambridge City Council member. "During the campaign, my father had left me to my own devices, but when it was over, he pointed out that I had taken my own neighborhood for granted. He was right: I had received a tremendous vote in the other sections of the city, but I hadn't worked hard enough in my own backyard. 'Let me tell you something I learned years ago,' he said. 'All politics is local.'"

Tip's father was, of course, right. Most everything in life now is local to some degree. Yet, ever increasingly, most everything has a global dimension as well. Higher education clearly is no exception. Online higher education is progressively becoming more local and more global. A colleague from India commented in a class we were taking together at Harvard, "All is local; all is global. My friend, everything is *glocal.*"

Online universities, as well as traditional venues of higher education, are increasingly partnering, on a global scale, with both the private and public sector. The globalization of higher education provides incredible opportunities for learners and faculty to better understand diverse cultures, norms, customs, and practices. It offers each of us a chance to grow in ways previously unknown. It also presents unprecedented opportunities to build lasting professional relationships. Frankly, the Internet is changing the planet into a borderless educational community where learning and networking are at your fingertips.

Chapter

3

Will My Online Degree Be Respected?

If you are going to invest your valuable time and money on a graduate degree, you surely will want to make certain you are receiving a worthy return on this investment. You may be concerned that web-based universities or programs are held in lesser regard than equivalent traditional based programs. While this clearly was the case not that many years ago, online degree programs now are perceived to be current, demanding, applicable, and respected in a world of rapid change and growth. There is good reason for this.

Online courses often are developed by experts in curriculum design and seasoned veterans from the *real* world who make certain the course concepts and materials are immediately applicable to a real world setting. This high degree of quality, relevance, and applicability is a tremendous asset that employers recognize and appreciate in their workforce. Indeed, learners with web-based degrees increasingly are finding a workplace that welcomes the initiative and self-reliance inherent in an online learning environment.

Vicky Philips noted a study conducted in 2000 concerning the acceptance of online degrees in corporate America that showed nearly 80 percent of private sector managers agreed that web-based programs are as valuable as traditional programs. This represented an almost 30 percent increase in private sector acceptance from a similar 1989 study. Philips indicated that this level of acceptance reaches 90 percent if the university is well-known or comes from a well-known state system such as those from California, Texas, and Maryland. That study was completed over ten years ago. I strongly suspect the level of acceptance has continued at a rapid rate.

Just look at the acceptance across the United States military. According to the Distance Education and Training Council, the Department of Defense spent more than $474 million on tuition assistance for higher education in FY 2008, and nearly two thirds of this amount went towards web-based learning! At the present rate of growth, online education will comprise three-fourths of the military's higher education funding in the coming year.

It also helps that big name universities, such as Harvard and the University of California at Berkley, are now offering online courses. As colleges rich in tradition with a reputation for academic rigor and integrity embrace online learning, the distinctions between web-based and face-to-face learning continue to blur. In fact, a recent Sloan Consortium study found that most Chief Academic Officers consider the quality and value of web-based instruction equal to or superior to that of traditional brick and mortar settings.

This level of acceptance within traditional higher education was exemplified when Capella University won the prestigious 2010 Council for Higher Education Accredi-

2010 CHEA Award

Outstanding Institutional Practice in Student Learning Outcomes

tation (CHEA) Award. CHEA is a national advocate and institutional voice concerning university accreditation and quality assurance to the public, academia, U.S. Congress, and U.S. Department of Education. This was the first time an online university has received this award. "Capella University is a leader in accountability in higher education. Their work in student learning outcomes exemplifies the progress that institutions are making through the implementation of comprehensive, relevant and effective initiatives," said CHEA President Judith Eaton.

Clearly accreditation, recognition, and reputation carry the day with regard to value of the university or program. Yet, ultimately, the worth and measure of a web-based degree rests on the continued rigor demanded by online faculty and programs as well as the commitment and contributions of those learners who have gone before you. Let me provide my experience regarding the first measure.

Programmatic Academic Rigor

While numerous faculty members at the FBI Academy today are working towards their doctorates in both traditional and online environments, this was not always the case. A colleague of mine was attending the University of Virginia working on his doctorate while I was attending Capella working on mine. Another peer and my boss were working on their doctorates from Virginia Tech. Another colleague was working on her doctorate from Virginia Commonwealth University. You can imagine the grief I took in those days simply because people did not understand and fully grasp what online learning from a reputable institution involved. However, my peers' paradigms changed over time by just watching the rigor and demands of my program. There actually came a tipping point where I honestly believe they started feeling sorry for me because my program was so rigorous. One of my colleagues would have to write a 15 page paper. I would have to write a 35 page paper. Another peer would submit a paper that paid negligible attention to proper citations and references. My papers would get crucified if APA format and style was not pristine. I vividly recall a long time Ph.D. telling me one day that when he earned his doctorate, he didn't have to go through a fraction of what I was experiencing.

My point here is simple. As long as online faculty and programs continue to hold learners accountable and demand excellence, acceptance and even admiration for web-based degrees will continue to increase.

It's Up To You

The second measure I mentioned was the continued contribution of online graduates. In any post-graduation endeavor, the three letters -P H D - will get you in the door. They will give you credibility... but only for a while. Ultimately, you have to earn your own keep and establish credibility for yourself. For example, when I present to various groups, the fact that I am an FBI Agent and have Ph.D. beside my name provides some measure of credibility. Yet, in a two hour presentation, this only lasts about two minutes. It is up to me to earn their respect from that point. I can substantiate the credibility I brought to the presentation, or I can blow it in just two simple minutes. This anecdote has implications in everything we do. If you want your online degree to be respected and valued, then you have to earn it every day. The higher you go in your education, the more responsible you are for your success. As with everything in life, you get what you put into it. Hold your head high and be confident because you know the rigor you experienced. Hold yourself to a different level with regard to expertise and character, and finally, contribute to make the world a better place.

Ask Online Alumni

As discussed in Chapter 1, the literature is full of studies that indicate no real differences with academic outcomes and learning between traditional and online programs. In fact, many studies show an increase in educational outcomes from online learning. These studies offer savvy employers a real glimpse into the rigor and value of online learning.

Another very important assessment tool that provides verification of the value of online degrees is the survey of online alumni. Information from alumni has the powerful potential to change university policy and curriculum. It also has the capacity to affect employer paradigms. Kendall and Pogue (2006) found in their research that 90% of online graduates would earn their degree through a web-based program if they had a choice to do it again. They also asked alumni to discuss their employment situations after graduation with regard to promotions and pay increases. Twenty percent responded that they received a promotion or salary increase with their current employer, and 18% said they earned a promotion or salary increase with a different employer after graduating from their web-based program. Overall, the participants earned, on average, a 39% increase in salary.

As alumni assessment is increasingly gaining in significance with regard to determining the true value of an education, research such as this provides substantive evidence that online graduates positively appraise their educational experiences likewise to graduates of traditional brick and mortar schools. In addition, this research provides evidence that employers are accepting web-based programs in a similar light as traditional programs.

> *During the past decade, online learning has begun to weave into the fabric of higher education and has become the fastest growing segment. All indications are that this growth will continue.*
>
> *~Peter McPherson*
> *President*
> *Association of Public and Land-grant Universities*

Final Thoughts

I do not want paint a picture that online programs are playing on a completely level field with regard to everyone's perceptions. Doubters, naysayers, and people who crave the status quo are bountiful in every aspect of human connectivity. However, the respect and value of online degrees has progressed significantly in the past few years. The line between how each person elects to learn through campus based delivery, an online format, or a blended combination is blurring to a point where the debate over quality will soon be a moot point.

Part

II

All Universities are not Created Equal

Critical Issues in Valuing a Degree

In this section we will look at what makes a university great. We will explore accreditation and the fraudulent world of diploma mills. But even if we start with a foundation that the university is legitimately accredited, all universities still are not created equal. There are numerous elements to a quality institution such as its reputation, faculty, and customer service. There are even specific program considerations that should be investigated. Maybe the university is accredited and has a sound reputation, but the particular program or certification you are interested in is not recognized by the appropriate association or state agency that grants licensure. For example, degrees in psychology are plentiful in online academia, but not all of these programs are recognized by the American Psychological Association or some states towards licensure as a psychologist. This section is designed to help you understand critical issues associated with your selection of an educational institution; in the end, however, you are the only one who can decide which university is best equipped to handle your individual needs.

Chapter

4

What Distinguishes a Great Online Program?

There are many components of an outstanding institution of higher learning. You may want to know how long the university has existed. While age means little in and of itself, particular in this new world of web-based higher education, age still may provide some insight into the stature of the university. In other words, is it a fly-by-night operation or one that has established itself in the academic community? What is the university's commitment to technological infrastructure? Who are their faculty? Is the university accredited by a legitimate regional and acknowledged accreditation association? Of course, the most important question you should ask: Is the university respected? The character and reputation of the university are the most important qualities you should consider.

Quality and Reputation

Right now, I am typing in the waiting room of a hospital about an hour and a half from my home. There are several other hospitals closer. My son is having a small procedure, and this is where the best specialist in this field practices. I am confident in the doctor's abilities because of his years of experience in the field, his reputation among people my wife and I know, and the fact that other physicians say this guy is the man! When you choose a physician, particularly a specialist, what do you use to base your decision? Location may play a small role. Whether they accept your insurance surely plays a role. Yet, I guarantee the most important factor you consider is the reputation of the doctor. What do other doctors say about him? What do your friends and work associates say? You may even call the state medical board. Regardless of how you do your homework, it all really boils down to reputation.

> *No change of circumstances can repair a defect of character.*
>
> ~*Ralph Waldo Emerson*

Beyond what type of degree you have (BS, MS, JD, MD, PhD, etc.), the first question employers, colleagues, and those you will interact with on a daily basis ask is, "Where did you get your degree?" Your response means everything. There is a night and day difference between saying "Harvard University" as opposed to "Global Transnational University for the Inept!" Universities take their reputation seriously and so should you. Your university, your program, must represent quality. It needs to be respected for your degree to be respected. While accreditation is the first step in determining quality, reputation goes well beyond the formal accreditation process required to achieve such recognition.

There is one caveat with regard to reputation. Reputation, whether good or bad, is not always deserved. As Abraham Lincoln observed,

"Character is like a tree and reputation its shadow. The shadow is what we think it is; the tree is the real thing." You always have to consider the source when making your judgments.

> *Associate with men of good quality if you esteem your own reputation; for it is better to be alone than in bad company.*
>
> ~*George Washington*

Quality of Life

When you commit to a university, you are committing years of your life. The quality of those years is a big deal. My experience as a student, whether face-to-face or online, was that access to information makes or breaks a student and makes or breaks a university. When learners need help, even with the smallest things, a friendly voice or information packed website can make all the difference in the quality the student's educational life. Trust me, no matter how well structured and credible the institution and program, there will be occasions when you need help. It may be computer problems, access to courseroom issues, Blackboard challenges, a policy or procedure you need help with, or assistance navigating the library. The extent to which universities provide quick, professional, and user friendly services makes all the difference in the world to your ability to succeed and thrive in graduate school.

Online universities with significant investments in infrastructure and people far surpass a traditional university's capacity to provide around the clock support. However, keep in mind that not all online universities and programs are created equal. The level of support provided to learners varies considerably from university to university. Take a look at websites from various universities. While fancy websites can be both attractive and misleading, a quality website with multiple links to a variety of academic and institutional information offers a glimpse into the university's commitment to learner support. Talk with school representatives to gauge their friendliness, responsiveness, and professionalism. Of course, beware here. Universities, traditional and web-based, put their most outgoing and persistent people in recruiting. A warm welcome does not necessarily reflect how the university will treat you once you're enrolled. As mentioned before, possibly the best way to ascertain true customer service and support is to talk with current students or graduates about their experiences regarding quality of life. Ask to talk to a current student or alumni when you're considering a university. These current and graduated students can answer questions in ways that non-students simply can not.

Let me share a little parable with you that a former colleague once shared with me. A bull and a turkey were in a field. The turkey kept running and jumping in the air. The bull asked, "Hey turkey, what are you doing?" The turkey responded, "I'm trying to fly?" This went on for several weeks to no avail. Finally, the bull walked over to the turkey and said, "Look, if you want to fly, you need to eat my dung that's lying all over the field." Of course, the turkey thought the bull was crazy and had nothing else to do with him for several weeks. As time passed though, the turkey became increasingly desperate to fly. With no available options, the turkey gave in and ate some of the dung. Wow...the turkey flew three feet off the ground! The next day saw six feet. Every day brought new heights for the turkey. One beautiful morning, the turkey took flight and landed on the tallest tree in the neighboring forest...where he was immediately shot by the landowner. The moral to the story...

BS may get you to the top, but it won't keep you there ☺

High flying recruiters are no different. They may be able to get you in the door, but eventually they will have to be able to back up their promises. The solid universities, with a strong reputation, will proudly back up every word, but the less than reputable schools simply will not be able to. Do your homework first and avoid being the turkey!

Enrollment Numbers

The importance of enrollment numbers in higher education depends on the context. Size of the student body is a very important factor that can be linked to effective learning in the classroom. For example, classes with fewer students generate stimulating discussion, which is at the heart of adult learning. Online schools typically aim for no more than 20 students per class session, and many have less. This is hardly the case in traditional universities.

It is important to note that the size of the university's entire student population does not indicate or guarantee the quality of the university. It may be tempting to rationalize that a college with huge numbers of students equates with excellence. Sometimes colleges with large enrollment are outstanding. But small universities are just as likely to have exceptional programs. The University of Maryland University College (UMUC) boasts over 90,000 students in their programs. The University of Phoenix reports a student population over 250,000 with nearly 23,000 faculty members. Walden University's website asserts, "When you enroll at Walden University, you join an international community that includes more than 270,000 students studying online..." While student enrollment clearly reflects popularity, it is not necessarily an indication of excellence. These universities have stellar reputations. However, the number of students attending these schools is not a credible criterion to base your assessment of excellence. You have to look beyond enrollment numbers.

Faculty

The last time my family moved, the first two things we considered when determining where we would buy a home were the commuting times to work and, of course, the costs of housing in different areas. Yet, as important as these two issues were, the most important factor in our housing equation was the school system that our children would attend. I know many of you have done the same thing. One thread that is common among every parent reading this book is that the needs and well-being of our children come first.

So, how did we know which school system was the best? We started asking around...a lot. As we have already discussed, reputation is critical in everything. We also assembled statistics from the state that showed percentages of students going on to college after graduation from various school districts. We looked at the average SAT scores among schools. We looked at awards the schools had won. Yet, some of the most important qualities we assessed were related to the faculty. What was the student/teacher ratio? What percentage of the faculty had graduate degrees? What was the average tenure of faculty members in that school system? As the faculty of my children's potential school mattered, so too should the faculty at your prospective university.

> *The success of any online endeavor in higher education rests with the learner and more importantly on the shoulders of the learners' faculty.*
>
> *Debbie Beebe, Ph.D.*
> *Capella graduate*
> *Class of 2007*

Most universities will give you access to their faculty directory. Take a look to see what institutions faculty members attended to earn their degrees. Consider the real world experience their faculty members have in the field they are teaching. You may want to see how long they have been teaching or assess their publishing record. The bottom line is that a university's faculty composition can reveal a tremendous amount of insight into the credibility of the university and the specific programs of interest to you.

Course/Curriculum Development

In my view, the best graduate programs exploit the experiences, skills, and expertise of both course design experts and faculty members. Unlike many traditional universities, online colleges often separate the development of courses from the actual task of instruction. In fact, in many web-based courses, actual instructors may have nothing to do with the design. Conversely, some course designers may seek to teach the courses they have developed. Faculty, therefore, bring expertise in two key areas of the curriculum to the learning experience: Subject matter expertise (SMEs) and instructional expertise.

Course development at Capella shares some of these elements but in an extremely efficient way. It is clearly a team effort with expertise and review on several levels. The team comprises a SME, course developer, course producer, and multi-media experts as well as a feedback and review process from faculty chairs. The entire process is well organized, very professional, and provides a world-class process for course development.

Another critical component of curriculum development is the attention to delivery and presentation. As we have discussed previously, different people have different learning preferences. The best graduate courses use a variety of pedagogies in an effort to make learning as exciting and powerful as possible. The aged teaching paradigm of lecture based instruction is not apparent in online learning. A dull mass lecture is replaced with a dynamic *discussion* among a small number of students and faculty using all sorts of techniques and tools. The online courses I have designed and taught contained multiple weekly discussions, individual assignments, and a wide diversity of multi-media. I have interviewed experts in the field and had the interviews incorporated into courses. Online courses may contain simple quizzes or flash cards, or they may contain very complicated and extensive multi-media presentations. Some students learn better

> *Today's teachers at every level, from kindergarten through graduate school, must have new knowledge in wide areas – not just their own subjects and the new technology, but in such matters as new learning styles, as well.*
>
> *~Sara Dulaney Gilbert*
> *Author*
> *How to be a Successful*
> *Online Student*

by reading, others by listening, others by discussion, others by doing, and the list goes on. Yet, not all online programs are multi-media savvy and invest time and money at similar levels in course design.

Talk to learners at the schools you are considering about their courses and the curriculum you are evaluating. Alumni and fellow students can be your best source of accurate information. Many online programs have free sample courses you may take just to get a feel for how they work. Regardless of the way you assess quality, taking a hard look at the school's curriculum design process is a wise investment of time and energy.

Final Thoughts

Choosing the right university and program is one of the most important decisions you will ever make. It will help you or haunt you throughout your entire life. I hope this section has provided a little insight into the most important qualities you should consider. Ask good questions. Do your homework and choose wisely. You are the only one that can choose the right university for your specific needs. You no longer have to settle for less than you really want. The options and opportunities are right at your fingertips! The following table with tips and advice was adapted from *Online Colleges and Degrees* with their permission.

Choosing an Online College

© 2007 Online Colleges and Degrees

1. Don't be lazy. Investigate and request information from several online colleges.

2. Don't eliminate an online college or university just because it is not an institution whose name you recognize.

3. Don't be afraid to ask questions. In fact, put together a list of questions before talking with admissions representatives.

4. Don't rule out a college immediately because of cost. Financial aid, credit for life experience, scholarships, and tuition payment plans may make a college or university far more affordable than it appears to be.

5. Don't "blow off" any admissions representatives who may call you. Take advantage of the opportunity they offer you to learn more about their programs.

6. Don't trust your memory. Take good notes when you read college brochures and speak with admissions representatives.

7. Do not be discouraged or intimidated by financial aid forms. Most online colleges have staff members who will be happy to help you.

8. Do not settle on the first seemingly appropriate online degree program you discover.

9. Don't keep your interest in continuing your education a secret. If you talk to friends, family members, and colleagues they can share their experiences and offer you important encouragement and support.

Chapter

5

Accreditation & Diploma Mills

The goal of accreditation is to ensure that education provided by institutions of higher education meets acceptable levels of quality.

U.S. Department of Education

What's the Big Deal with Accreditation?

> *Accreditation is a signal to students and the public that an institution or program meets at least minimal standards for its faculty, curriculum, student services and libraries.*
>
> ~*Judith S. Eaton*
> *President*
> *Council for Higher*
> *Education Accreditation*

Accreditation in the United States is a voluntary process whereby institutions submit for an evaluation of the quality of their entire institution or a specific program. Accreditation is the first and foremost standard to which learners, faculty, other universities, the government, and employers look when determining the value of your degree. There are some non-accredited schools that do a fine job of education. These are okay for students *if* they know what they are getting into and are willing to potentially devote years of their life to an endeavor that may not be recognized from a professional perspective. Accreditation means everything in the world of higher education!

There are numerous implications associated with accreditation. Many employers will not hire you if your degree is not from a regionally accredited institution. Many employers who offer tuition assistance will not pay for courses taken at a university that is not accredited. Non-accredited colleges are not eligible to participate in government backed student loan or grant programs. More importantly, courses taken at a non-accredited university will not be eligible for transfer to an accredited school. This has significant implications if you decide to further your education with a graduate degree but obtained your undergraduate degree from a university lacking proper accreditation.

Potential legal implications also exist with regard to claiming a legitimate degree if you did not attend an accredited school. The

Department of Education (http://ope.ed.gov/accreditation) offers, "In most U.S. state jurisdictions, falsification of a claim to have studied at or graduated from a recognized school or institution is punishable by revocation of licenses, fines, imprisonment, or a combination." In some jurisdictions, such as Oregon, it is illegal to gain advantage in getting a job or promotion by using a degree from an unlicensed institution.

The central and most prevalent challenge with regard to attending non-accredited schools is that such a degree lacks recognition with regard to academic rigor, value of the degree awarded, and typically carries minimal or no credibility in the real world of professional practice. You may or may not have worked very hard for the degree. You may or may not have spent a significant amount of time and money towards the degree. It makes no difference. Without accreditation, the ultimate value of the degree is questionable.

The following table, adapted from information provided by the U.S. Department of Education, provides a more in depth view of the important role of accreditation.

Some Functions of Accreditation

1. Verifying that an institution or program meets established standards;

2. Assisting prospective students in identifying acceptable institutions;

3. Assisting institutions in determining the acceptability of transfer credits;

4. Protecting an institution against harmful internal and external pressure;

5. Creating goals for self-improvement of weaker programs and stimulating a general raising of standards among educational institutions;

6. Involving the faculty and staff comprehensively in institutional evaluation and planning;

7. Establishing criteria for professional certification and licensure and for upgrading courses offering such preparation; and

8. Providing one of several considerations used as a basis for determining eligibility for Federal assistance.

Who Accredits?

Contrary to how this issue is addressed in many other countries, accreditation in the United States is neither conducted by the U.S. Department of Education or any government agency nor is it conducted by the Council for Higher Education Accreditation (CHEA). Instead, private associations are responsible for this review. As such, accreditation represents a complex and decentralized system of quality review (Eaton, 1996). Though the government or CHEA do not offer accreditation to schools, they do provide accreditation for the private associations charged with that responsibility.

While there are several types of accreditation, the two most respected are *regional* accreditation, for an entire university or college, and *programmatic* or *specialized* accreditation, for specific programs within a university. In addition to academic rigor, regional accrediting associations evaluate qualities such as administration, financial constancy, learner support, and constituent relationships. A programmatic accrediting agency assesses the quality of specific programs such as law (American Bar Association) or medicine (American Medical Association) within the university. Generally, these two types of accreditation compliment each other. Most traditional universities of sound character and reputation will be regionally accredited as well as specific programs offered by the university that are appropriate for program accreditation.

This is not to suggest that some non-regional or non-programmatic accrediting agencies do not offer value. In fact, the U.S. Department of Education recognizes numerous national accreditation agencies. For example, the Distance Education and Training Council (DETC) is a well-known national accrediting association focusing on distance education universities. Yet, even with the rigor and stellar reputation of the DETC, programs accredited by the DETC are not as regularly accepted by regionally accredited universities.

My point is simple. I would not associate myself with a non-regionally accredited university either as a student or faculty member. While my feelings may change in the future with the increasing acceptance of some national accreditation associations, clearly regional accreditation is the gold standard by which I strongly suggest you measure your school and program!

There are six regional accreditation associations, each distinct with their own websites that provide a wealth of information, and each enjoying reciprocity with the other five agencies.

Regional Accreditation Associations

- The Middle States Association of Colleges and Schools, Middle States Commission on Higher Education   www.msche.org

- New England Association of Schools and Colleges, Commission on Institutions of Higher Education www.neasc.org

- The North Central Association of Colleges and Schools, The Higher Learning Commission www.ncahigherlearningcommission.org

- The Northwest Association of Schools and Colleges, Northwest Commission on Colleges and Universities www.nwccu.org

- The Southern Association of Colleges and Schools, Commission on Colleges www.sacs.org

- The Western Association of Schools and Colleges www.wasc.org

---

Diploma and Accreditation Mills

Fly-by-night and less than reputable institutions of higher learning, as well as fraudulent accreditation agencies, have existed for many years, possibly as far back as the 1800s. Yet, the appearance of these *universities* and bogus accrediting agencies seems to have exploded onto the scene in recent years. This largely is due to the advent of online learning in higher education. As web-based higher education offers expanded opportunities for students, it also offers increased opportunities for those wishing to perpetrate fraud and deceit.

The Council for Higher Education Accreditation (CHEA) offers the following definition of diploma mills, closely adopted from Webster's Dictionary: "An institution of higher education operating without supervision of a state or professional agency and granting diplomas which are either fraudulent or because of the lack of proper standards worthless." Simply stated, diploma mills are inferior or sham institutions that typically confer degrees with very little or no work. The worst type simply provides an official looking diploma and transcripts in exchange for money. Other diploma mills require some work from the learner but clearly not with the expected quantity, quality, or rigor normally associated with a legitimate degree. Either way, diploma mills devalue legitimate degrees and represent the height of injustice to every student who has devoted significant time, money, and energy into earning an accredited degree.

Diploma mills have drawn substantial attention from all aspects of academia, private companies, government agencies, the media, and Congress. In 2004, at the request of Congress, the Government Accountability Office (GAO) attempted to evaluate the extent to which federal dollars were used to pay diploma mills on behalf of federal employees. The GAO determined that over 500 federal employees received degrees from diploma mills, including 28 senior level executives. Interestingly, the GAO surmised that their data was severely understated.

> *OPM policy is absolutely clear. Bogus degrees from so called diploma mills may not be used to qualify for federal jobs or salaries. The American people expect their public servants to be honest and forthcoming.*
>
> ~Kay Coles James
> Director
> Office of Personnel Management

How Can I Tell Between the Good and the Bad?

For students who enroll today only, we will provide a framed diploma, official transcripts, and three letters of recommendation from your professors. For an additional $100.00, your transcripts will reflect the honors of your choice.

Bachelor's, master's, and doctoral degrees available in any field of your choosing with no courses, books to read, or exams.

Earn an accredited Ph.D. in three months. Don't let all those years of valuable experience go to waste. We appreciate what life has taught you, and we reflect that in our degree requirements.

Yeah, right...Always remember, if it sounds too good to be true, it probably is!

There are two types of people who use diploma mills. The first are the ignorant suckers that just do not know what they are buying. Unfortunately, this probably happens quite a bit. These students visit the mill's website, are impressed with its quality and appearance, and even note the comments in italics that provide the name of the accreditation agency that accredited the university. What these potential students do not know, of course, is that the accrediting agency was just as bogus as the university. Indeed, many of these fictitious accrediting agencies are simply creations of the degree mills. When students enroll in such a diploma mill, they find out too late that there is no quality education attached to the diploma that arrives in the mail.

More often than not, it is the second type of person who *attends* a diploma mill. These people fully understand the university is not accredited, and that the work load and time requirements are considerably less than with legitimate programs. Yet, they are willing to engage in deception in order to pad their resume. The good news is that, in my experience, such professional fraud does come to an end sooner or later, and the consequences are devastating.

Because you are reading a book on how to successfully navigate grad school...a book with chapters on APA and scholarly writing, plagiarism, and research ethics, I feel confident you do not fall into this second category. So, how do good folks like you tell the difference between the legitimate and scam universities and accreditation agencies? One of the easiest ways is to consult the Department of Education's website at www.ed.gov. CHEA also has a very informative website at www.chea.org. Beyond these resources, the following table offers some suggestions to consider.

Watch out for universities that...

1. Are not regionally accredited!

2. Use language other than *accreditation* such as *currently pursuing accreditation, authorized, chartered, licensed,* or *approved.*

3. Use institutional names similar to well-known universities.

4. Place dramatic attention on affordability.

5. Place undue emphasis on the length (shortness) of the program requirements.

6. Offer degrees solely based on life experience.

7. Pay little attention to selection rigor...everyone who applies gets in.

8. Have a very small selection of degrees with vague requirements.

9. Market themselves solely as a religious organization.

10. Say accreditation is a complex and vague process that is not really needed in the United States.

Part
III

The Heart of
Online Education

Navigating the
Courseroom

Part III begins our journey towards graduation with a look at the Courseroom. The Courseroom is the heart of most online education programs as it serves as the classroom as well as the primary vehicle of communication among peers and the instructor. While Capella University serves as the broad setting for these next chapters, the strategies espoused here should be of worth to students in nearly all online degree programs regardless of the university or degree.

Chapter

6

The Truth About Graduate School

Nothing will ever take the place of persistence and hard work - Talent will not - There is nothing more common than the unsuccessful person with talent - Genius will not, for unrewarded genius is almost a proverb - Education alone will not, for the world is full of education failures - Persistence and hard work alone are omnipotent - persistent people will always begin their success where others end in failure.

~President Calvin Coolidge

Before we get into the specifics of online learning, we need to establish one major parameter. The following chapters are about savvy and navigation. Countless books offer get-rich-quick advice. Plenty more exist to tell us how to invest our hard earned money and win every time. Thousands of books on losing weight fast grace the shelves of our local book stores. And there are more than a few books offering surefire ways to get As in every class. But you and I know better. Once again…If it's too good to be true, it probably is. Earning your degree, whether online or in a face-to-face environment, is a challenging endeavor. There are no easy ways or short cuts to earning a legitimate degree from a reputable university.

I first started my doctoral journey at Temple University in Philadelphia. Ultimately, because of work demands surrounding the events of September 11, 2001, and a transfer to the Washington, DC area in early 2002, I was forced to leave Temple. For many of the reasons and benefits discussed in Chapter 2, I eventually enrolled in Capella University. Although at Temple a very short time, I learned probably the most important lesson any doctoral student can be taught.

The first week of class, the professor assigned 500 pages of reading. I almost fell out of my chair. Did he not know we were working adults with real lives? Well, the fact was that out of the eleven students in the course, only two of us had full time careers. The other nine pretty much had their entire day to focus on their studies. In fact, most had offices in the building as they were on a stipend from the university. With this in mind, I kept my mouth closed and pushed ahead. Weeks two, three, and four brought the same thing – about 500 pages each week. I was dying a slow and very painful death. Then, for week five, the professor assigned almost 1000 pages to read…a beautiful assortment of book chapters and journal articles. My compatriot in pain and I marched to his office after class. I pleaded, "Professor, with all due respect, you're killing us. No human being can read 1000 pages in one week…much less students who have full time careers." I will never forget the Truth that he spoke. "Gentlemen, first let me explain doctoral level reading. Ph.D.s read for patterns and themes. They skim and learn to hone in on what's important and avoid what's not. But more importantly, I don't think you understand the amount of work ahead of you as a Ph.D. student." The professor then stood from behind his desk. He held his right hand about three feet off of the ground and said, "Here's the quantity of work for an Associate degree." He then moved his hand up a couple of inches and said, "Here's the amount of work for a Bachelor's degree." Again, he raised his hand up another few inches. "Here's the amount of work for a Master's degree." Then he climbed up on his chair, raised his right hand as far as it would go in the air and said, "Here's the amount of work for a Ph.D." This anecdote provides two lessons. Earning a Ph.D., with its associated high value and respect, truly takes a lot of hard work. Secondly, there are ways to read voluminous amounts of materials every week.

I do not want to paint a picture that achieving a bachelor's or master's degree is easy. Indeed, for working adults in particular, the challenges of any higher education program can be daunting. The truth about higher education, particularly at the doctoral level, is that there are no easy ways to earn your degree. Thus, I did end up reading thousands and thousands of pages of research and theory. I realized that pursuing a graduate degree as an adult learner with a family, job, and multitude of other responsibilities required tremendous sacrifice. And, I could do it in an online learning environment that allowed flexibility about when and how I would complete academic requirements. If you persevere as I did, I promise you will have no doubt about the worth of your efforts while you're achieving each milestone along the way.

Ji zoku shin

The Japanese term for perseverance is Ji zoku shin. It represents the spirit of *continuing* as opposed to beginning. Seido Karate Grandmaster Tadashi Nakamura observed, "It doesn't take much courage to begin on a new path. But how far are we willing to go with it? Do we have the spirit, the sincere attitude to continue on the path?" Perseverance, developing healthy attitudes, and avoiding procrastination are the fundamental keys to success. Understanding your university's landscape and expectations will help immensely, but the most important ingredients for success are sound habits.

> *Habit has everything to do with everything we do!*

The good news with habits is that they can offer us a well-defined paradigm with which we will use in everything we do. The bad news about habits is that they can offer us a well-defined paradigm with which we will use in everything we do! In other words, if we truly want to develop habits of perseverance and hard work, then we have to learn to control our habits instead of them controlling us. Although very difficult at times, good habits can be learned, and poor habits can be unlearned. As Henry James proclaimed, "The greatest discovery of our generation is that attitude is the most important ingredient in changing behavior." As we begin our journey towards graduation, I ask you to reflect upon the powerful message behind Sean Covey's poem, which he was kind enough to allow me to reprint on the following pages.

Who am I?

I am your constant companion.
I am your greatest helper or heaviest burden.
I will push you on ward or drag you down to failure.
I am completely at your command.
Half the things you do you might just as well run over to me
and I will be able to do them quickly and correctly.

I am easily managed – you must merely be firm with me.
Show me exactly how you want something done
and after a few lessons I will do it automatically.
I am the servant of all great individuals and,
alas, of all failures, as well.
Those who are great, I have made great.
Those who are failures, I have made failures.

I am not a machine, though I work with all the precision of a machine
plus the intelligence of a human.
You may run me for a profit or run me for ruin –
it makes no difference to me.

Take me, train me, be firm with me,
and I will place the world at your feet.
Be easy with me and I will destroy you.

Who am I?

I am Habit.

Chapter

7

FirstCourse

How Do I
Learn Online?

by

Ben Noah, Ph.D.

Capella University
School of Human Services
FirstCourse Lead Faculty

FirstCourse represents the first class learners attend with Capella University. It is content driven within the discipline of the learner's school and degree. In other words, the course takes the shape and feel of a normal class with normal content but is set in the context of the FirstCourse philosophy. For example, the School of Business may focus on developing a business perspective, while the School of Human Services may focus on human behavior and the life cycle – all under an umbrella of introducing learners to online learning at Capella. While FirstCourse is unique to Capella, many web-based programs follow a similar philosophy of providing learners an initial environment where they experience success and begin to develop habits necessary in their academic journey.

FirstCourse is taken very seriously at Capella. Only experienced faculty members of the highest caliber are afforded the opportunity to teach these courses. Many specific topics are addressed in the course such as plagiarism, courseroom etiquette (netiquette) and practices, and faculty and learner expectations. The heart of FirstCourse is similar to the mission of this book: To help learners understand online learning and what it takes to succeed. The purpose of this chapter is to highlight some of the more salient aspects of the FirstCourse experience.

First Things for FirstCourse

While it may seem obvious when thinking about how to get ready for the first course you will take, I recommend that you have your textbook and the *APA Manual* in hand before your classes start. As an instructor, it never ceases to amaze me the number of learners who contact me half way through the course (after the first paper has been graded) saying they did not know they needed to use the *APA Manual* (*Publication Manual of the American Psychological Association, Fifth Edition*) even though it was clearly stated in the syllabus. Read the course syllabus several times to get a good feel for what is expected and keep it handy throughout the duration of the course. Faculty Expectations also should be read several times, printed, and referred to often. Please do not *walk* into the courseroom expecting everything to just fall in place. When in doubt about anything, ask your instructor. This is a good idea anytime – the more interaction with your instructor to seek clarification and answers to questions, the better.

Successful learners organize and maintain a work space for school. This should be *your* area and should be free from distractions (i.e., no TV). This can be an office, bedroom, shed in the back yard – whatever, as long as it has Internet access and affords you peace and quiet to do your work. If you have a significant other, the bedroom is great for this job – it insures you'll be getting enough sleep. Another good idea with this work area is to hang a big wall calendar with all of your assignment due dates in large, bold letters. You may even want to place occasions like birthdays and anniversaries on the calendar. This may save you a big headache later.

Critical Thinking

At this level of education, there are words you want to avoid. Phrases and terms like "I think" and "I believe" are anathema to critical thinking as it is conceptualized in graduate academic settings. Critical thinking is moving beyond simple levels of self to verifiable scientific knowledge. You may have heard the phrase, "You are not allowed to have an opinion until you have a Ph.D." The genesis of this truth is in critical thinking.

You will hear of Bloom's Taxonomy from day one in your graduate education. Bloom's provides a view of critical thinking through a taxonomy of learning. However, it can take some time to fully understand what this taxonomy is all about. A shorter road to critical thinking is in becoming a skeptic. Prior to the scientific method, skepticism was the path to knowledge. The skepticism I'm referring to is not a modern version of that perspective which has come to more or less mean cynicism.

Healthy skepticism, rather, forms a normal and preferred route to knowledge. To be a skeptic in science is to be critical of information; to not take it as truth without first delving into information using critical thinking skills and insights. The FirstCourse actually focuses on the student's academic readiness and problem solving capabilities as they begin the graduate program recognizing that these steps represent significant progressions towards developing strong critical thinking skills.

> *The educated man is as superior to the uneducated as the living are to the dead.*
> Aristotle

The following acronym from Wayne Bartz may provide a little context: *CRITIC*.

C: *Claim* - Is what is being proposed scientifically observable and measurable?

R: *Role* of the claimant – This is the issue of "says who?"

I: *Information* backing the claim – Are there multiple sources with the same information, or is it a single case?

T: *Test* – Can the claim be tested to weed-out errors in thought or biases?

I: *Independent* testing – Are there multiple sources of reliable, unbiased research to back the claim?

C: *Cause* proposed – Is the claim consistent with known laws and paradigms?

Time Management

The two biggest mistakes I see learners make after they've enrolled in an online course is getting behind in their assignments and then not letting their instructor know they're in trouble. Reality tells us that it is difficult to find enough time for course work on top of an already busy schedule. Time management, therefore, while certainly a challenge for adults who are juggling school, community, work, and family responsibilities, is an essential skill set for the online student!

Time management is a well known and important skill set applicable throughout the lifespan. Like money management, the first step in time management is self-awareness. How do you spend your time? Consider keeping a log for one week to track exactly how you spend your time. Write down the time you begin and end an activity. Briefly describe the activity. Be honest! Next, analyze your time log. Summarize and categorize the amount of time spent on each type of activity. I assure you that you will be surprised about how you use your time.

Next, develop a new daily schedule to maximize your time. Take into consideration where certain tasks fit best into your day as well as when you are at your best for certain tasks, such as studying. Consider grouping similar tasks together for efficiency and set aside time for doing uninterrupted work. Write down your new routine or schedule and post it where you will see it! Be flexible. Revisit and revise your schedule as needed.

Strategies for your new routine:

- Prioritize your tasks. Which ones are high priorities and which ones can wait if necessary? Prioritize your people contacts, your telephone calls, and your email replies. Do this first thing in the morning or the night before so that you are ready to go in the morning.
- Build "cushion time" into your schedule so that you have some flexibility and "catch up" time.
- Take time for yourself. Schedule "me time" even if it is only 15 minutes each day. Build "me time" into your normal routine. Listen to your favorite music or exercise. Or take a walk with a friend or colleague to maintain and build relationships and burn off lunch.
- Structure your telephone time. Set aside certain times of the day to accept, initiate, and return calls. The best time to accept incoming calls is just prior to lunch or at the end of the work day because the other person probably will not want to spend much time on the phone. The best time for initiating or returning calls is early in the morning just before or after lunch or late in the day. Plan in advance what you need to cover during the call. At the beginning of the call, you might say, "I have about 10 minutes to

spend with you, now. If we don't finish, we can schedule another time."

- Do not procrastinate. Tackle the unpleasant tasks first. (This includes taking out the trash.)
- If necessary, negotiate a different work schedule with your employer (longer hours and fewer days; work-at-home days).
- Reduce interruptions by creating stronger boundaries around work, study, personal, and family time. Let people know when you can and cannot be interrupted.

> *It is not the technology or course content that will sink your boat;*
> *it is time management, procrastination, and the normal issues of life.*

You only have 24 hours in a day; therefore, under-promise and over-deliver! Learn to say "NO." Do not over-commit yourself. Develop a formula for making commitments. For example, one parent created the following formula: One activity for me; one commitment to my community; one to my church; one to husband, and one to each child. Sometimes, two commitments were fulfilled with one activity. Each child was allowed two activities in addition to church activities. Activities were re-evaluated at the beginning of each school year. If anyone added an activity or commitment, they had to drop another one. They quickly learned to prioritize their time and other resources!

Procrastination

Beyond time management, procrastination has to be the biggest reason for failure to accomplish goals. It always is easier to do something tomorrow, but then it doesn't get done tomorrow either. The quickest way to get caught in the procrastination trap is to doubt yourself. It is amazing how much time is wasted and how much stress is induced by listening to our "devils of despair." Becoming too concerned about GPA also may cause hesitancy in doing your work. These kinds of "I can't" thoughts can freeze you in place.

The antidote to "I can't" is to keep your *eye on the prize*. Write a large framed message to yourself with your goals on it and put it right where you do you school work. Stay in touch with your cohort mates and be a constant support to one another. If you really want to be creative, do what I did. Buy your tam and put it on your computer monitor. As much money as that cost, I wasn't going to stop short of the goal.

Some time back I got an e-mail from a learner who was in a frantic panic about her coursework and the doubt devils were moving in. As I read and re-read her e-mail, a poem came to mind – I call it *Three Little Letters*.

Three little letters floating in the air,
What do they mean?
Why should I care?

Some people say I'm ADD
My mind is always racing like a bee
I fidget, I flee
I really think I'm OCD
Perfection is really a quest for me
If I can't get it right, I drop to my knees

GPA, what should it be
A goal for me?
Or, a mark of where I've been?

ABD is a definite possibility –
If I take the OCD to seriously
Or, let the GPA be the end of me

Of all the three little letters
In the world for me
The only ones that counts are – P H D !

Life Issues

Stressful life issues are simply a given these days, and graduate school does not stand still for them. Work, family, community, all compete with school for our time. There will be plenty of occasions in which you feel like a juggler with too many balls in the air. Some simple things can help to keep you on track.

Have a long talk with those you live with at your home – even the dog. Children may have a hard time starting off understanding why mom or dad is unavailable. One way that I overcame this was to have my daughter do her homework at the same time and in the same room where I did mine. After more than 10 years, she still calls this "special times." Talk to your spouse about your personal goals and also where you see the family in the dreams you're working to achieve.

Take a day off each week. Sunday was my day off. It was my time for family, church, and self-care. My family knew this and would not let me think of getting on the computer on "our" day. Illnesses and deaths will happen, and they never schedule themselves. When something this drastic happens, immediately let your instructor know. Faculty members tend to give considerable leeway if brought in early to a situation. If life becomes too stressful, do not be afraid or ashamed to take some time off from school. It is better to take a break and come back invigorated when your mind is ready to learn again. As final word on your academic journey – Always keep your instructor in the loop.

Chapter

8

APA & Graduate Writing

Graduate school assignments and papers come in many forms. For example, you may be asked to write a position, opinion, or research paper or any number of other types of papers. Regardless of the style of paper, two things remain constant. The first is that graduate assignments need to reflect the appropriate level of critical and creative thinking relative to the degree. We will talk more about this in the Blooms Taxonomy chapter in Part IV.

The second constant is that graduate papers need to be written with economy of words, accuracy, and consistency. Unless told otherwise, it should have a scholarly feel and format. This book, for example, is not a good example of scholarly writing. The tone is conversational and frequently uses colloquial phrases. Numerous quotes can be found throughout the various chapters. Many sentences start with *and* or *but*. Contractions are used throughout the book. In text citations are not provided with many quotations. Any of these characteristics would doom a graduate level paper. Following the writing style manual approved by your university or program is a very important step in learning how to write like a scholar.

While there are several very well known and respected writing manuals used in professional writing, APA and MLA are probably the most prevalent. APA, the affectionate acronym for the writing manual published by the American Psychological Association, is the dominant manual with programs focusing on social sciences, human services, psychology, and business. The MLA (Modern Language Association) style manual more commonly is used in programs focusing on liberal arts and humanities. Don't be surprised, however, to see Chicago as a preferred manual for many peer-reviewed journals.

APA as a Process

I will never forget the kind remark said to me by a professor in one of my early doctoral courses. I was frustrated with the comments I had received from her about my adherence to APA. Frankly, I only marginally saw the value of being APA compliant, and I sure was not picking it up very quickly. Heck, I had used MLA during grad school, and even

> *Knowing is a process,*
> *not a product.*
>
> *~Jerome Bruner*

that was ten years ago. Sensing my frustration, Dr. Stechschulte encouragingly offered, "Jeff, relax and just keep at it. It will come. Never forget... APA is a *process*." Learning APA is a process. It is an extremely important process for graduate learners in that it offers consistency with regard to mechanics, but more importantly, it provides a context for students to learn how to write concisely, precisely, and objectively.

Why Such a Fuss about APA?

In preparing for this book, I read several authors who, in one way or the other, advise students to make sure they find out what writing manual the professor wants. They continue that students will need to do this at least a week ahead of the assignment due date so they will know how to format their paper. Some authors mention getting style sheets from their professors so learners will be able to write their paper the correct way.

The truth is that this way of thinking and teaching is bizarre, misleading, and just plain incorrect. Learning APA and good writing is a long term process. Sound writing, particularly scholarly writing, is an art and skill set that will allow you to communicate clearly, express your thoughts smoothly and in a logical order, and offer a level of consistency in writing to your chosen field. You do not learn APA (or MLA or Chicago or any other manual) in a week. As nice as cheat sheets or style sheets are, they cannot replace a 450 word text or specific feedback from your professors.

APA is not just about citations and references. It is about presenting your thoughts in a coherent and consistent manner. By the time you get to the comprehensive exam phase of your doctoral program, APA should not be an issue. Yet, so often it is...We will talk more about that in the Comps chapter.

> *Over the years, the Publication Manual has grown by necessity from a simple set of style rules to an authoritative source on all aspects of scholarly writing, from ethics of duplicate publication to the word choice that best reduces bias in language.*
>
> *APA Manual 6th Edition*

Your instructors have a tremendous amount of discretion in their classes. Holding students accountable for adhering to APA is no different. Some professors know APA inside and out and believe very strongly that graduate learners must learn this style of writing. Some professors do not know APA very well themselves, thus do not push it on their students. My experience is that most professors are somewhere in the middle. But make no mistake, almost all faculty members hold students very accountable for good writing in the comprehensive exam.

A Few Tips

During the first week or two of each class, I offer my learners a list of common APA and writing issues that I see in courses and comprehensive exams. This list is provided on the following pages. Please keep in mind that the American Psychological Association (APA) revises their manual periodically. My comments are based on APA 6th Edition published in 2010. Lastly, you should be aware that even universities or departments who adhere to APA or any other style manual may have different requirements in some areas. So, it is very important to review your specific college or department's writing policy and give them what they want.

Clearly, this list is not exhaustive. Your individual instructors may have their own pet peeves or items of importance with regard to APA and scholarly writing. These are just a few that come to mind that I see give learners a hard time in their courses, comprehensive exam, and even the dissertation.

Common Writing and APA Issues
(In no particular order of importance)

- Title pages frequently are incorrect. Take a look on page 41 of the APA manual. You will notice differences between APA 5th and APA 6th Editions.

- Abstracts create problems for many learners. Abstracts need to be in the active voice in that they tell the reader what the paper does, not what it will do or did do. What the paper will do is the responsibility of the paper's introduction and did do is the responsibility of the conclusion. Use present tense with your results and past tense to describe your variables and tests. Please read pages 25-27 in the APA manual.

- 1" margins on all four sides of each page.

- Verbs agreeing – for example, 'should always go' should be 'always should go.'

- Make sure your verb tense also agrees...for example, if you start the sentence with present tense then you cannot use past tense later in the same sentence.

- Do not use quotation marks around words to give them emphasis. APA 6th does allow this, which is a change from the 5th, but still do not do it. Just use quotation marks when quoting someone.

- No place for single quotation marks in APA except on rare occasion. See the APA manual.

- Incorrect citations in text and incorrect referencing at the end of the paper are consistent problems. The APA manual easily can fix this.

Common Writing and APA Issues
(Continued)

- Make sure your citations have the corresponding reference at the end of the paper and conversely, make sure your references have been cited at least once in the paper.

- Bibliographies really do not exist in APA papers. Use a reference page instead.

- Quotations of 40 or more words have to be block quoted.

- APA actually frowns on quotes because graduate students should be able to synthesize and paraphrase in their own words. Only quote when the words are so unique that paraphrasing would substantively hurt the message.

- Do not use bullets or numbers in your lists. APA 6th allows for this but avoid them anyway. At this level, you should be able to paraphrase.

- When you do have a series of items in your writing, make sure to look at the APA manual for the proper way to do it.

- Headings are extremely important in presenting your ideas in a coherent and logical manner, but APA is very strict in how you format them. Look in the manual on pages 62-63.

- Avoid secondary sources to the extent possible. Graduate students go straight to the source instead of relying on other people's word.

- Two spaces after periods!!! This is big change from APA 5th Edition.

- No hyphens in APA.

Common Writing and APA Issues
(Continued)

- Never use contractions in formal writing... don't, can't, won't, etc.!!!

- Never start a sentence with a conjunction.... Or, But, And, etc.

- The majority of your references should be peer-reviewed such as scholarly journals or dissertations. Books are not prohibited in the slightest as there are many credible authors out there. Yet, be very careful using books as sources for your papers because anyone can write anything in book form.

- NEVER use Wikipedia for anything in any type of writing. Don't even let your children use it. While most of the information generally is correct, it is not reliable because anyone can change the content.

- Avoid colloquial terms and phrases such as ...he really stepped up to plate to... Scholarly papers have to stand on their own with regard to diverse audiences. An international student may not have a clue what stepped up to the plate means or even what have a clue means.

- I see typos all over the place in papers. This is absolutely unacceptable at the graduate level! Proofread, proofread, proofread!!!

- This is the big one – Plagiarism. PLEASE give credit (attribution) where credit is due. Professors spot plagiarism in two seconds, and mydropbox or safeassign or other services catch the rest. If you use someone's thoughts, give them credit!!!!! This is no joke ladies and gentlemen.

Clearly, this list is not exhaustive. Your individual instructors may have their own pet peeves or items of importance with regard to APA and scholarly writing. These are just a few that come to mind that I see give learners a hard time in their courses, comprehensive exam, and even the dissertation.

Final Thoughts

I once saw a faculty member at a colloquium use coffee as an analogy for APA. He said coffee is to writing, as the mug is to APA. You could take this comment to mean that content is more important than the mechanics and overall presentation, albeit both are important. In the context of his other remarks, I took it to mean that both sound content and presentation have to be present to have a successful paper. Coffee without a mug is empty hope. A mug without coffee is…well, just empty.

Having said this, I don't see too much value in asking whether the writing or content is more important in graduate school. Critical thinking and good writing skills are both critical. You have to have both for success in school and after graduation. A colleague at the FBI Laboratory Division told me the horror he felt when his first article submission to a peer-reviewed journal came back with the remarks… *"Writing is not at an acceptable level for this journal."* The editors never mentioned the content, which he said was based on years of sound research.

The bottom line is that if you cannot effectively communicate your thoughts at a scholarly level, your ideas, as wonderfully researched as they may be, never will get through to the reader. Readers will assume if you do not possess the commitment to learn how to write, you obviously do not possess the commitment to conduct proper research. The paper's credibility is severely devalued, which obviously devalues your credibility.

Chapter 9

Peer Review

And Other Acceptable Sources

One of the toughest concepts graduate students have comprehending is that their papers should be supported by evidence as opposed to anecdotes or their opinions. Of course, there may be an occasion where professors ask for an opinion paper, but even in that case, they more than likely will expect you to support your opinions with the insights from experts or empirical research. Recently, I returned a paper to a student without a grade and gave him the opportunity to conduct a rewrite because the writing was too colloquial and too opinionated. This was his first reply. "Dr. Green, I've heard this before from previous instructors. I'm just worried about losing my sense of self if I can't say what I know from my life experiences." I replied, "Call me and let's talk about graduate level writing. I also want to put you in touch with the writing center. But here's the deal in a nutshell.

If you're married to writing in a conversational tone based on your opinions, then you need to write a book instead of working on your Ph.D. Call me. We'll get through this together."

I have heard some professors tell students, "No one is interested in your opinions until you have *Ph.D.* after your name." I understand the point they are trying to make, but I think their presentation is a little misguided. Most professors are very interested in their students' opinions. Indeed, it drives our courseroom discussions and brings a sense of context to the theories and models we are discussing. Yet, unless told otherwise by your professors, make sure your opinions are objectively presented in the context of synthesis and evaluation, and that your conclusions are supported by scholarly sources. Frankly, your papers will need the acumen and insights of experts to provide evidence and support for your conclusions.

Different instructors have different guidelines concerning the number of citations and scholarly references you should use in your papers. I like to see, as a general rule of thumb, at least one citation per paragraph. Depending on the size of the paper, your professor may ask for 5 scholarly sources or 25 scholarly sources. Personally, I like to see about 15 in a 25 page paper. Again, most instructors are not looking for exact numbers. They just want to make sure your paper is thoroughly researched, contains a fairly wide breadth and depth of opinion and research, and that the paper used reputable sources. And please make sure you cite correctly, not just with the APA formatting, but also with the placement of the citation. Placing your citation at the end of the paragraph just does not work at the graduate level. This is more of a high school type of thing kids do to cover themselves from plagiarism. The problem is that this simply does not show critical thinking, which is requisite at this level. So try sandwiching your citations in the middle of the paragraph. The idea being that you offer an idea, support it with the literature (citation), then complete the paragraph with your own critical thinking (analysis, synthesis, evaluation) on the thought.

Scholarly Sources

Several types of sources are acceptable in graduate writing. Let's start with the most acceptable: *Scholarly* sources. Scholarly articles are original works. This infers that "they have not been previously published, that they contribute to the archive of scientific knowledge, and that they have been reviewed by a panel of peers" (APA 6th Edition, p. 225). Scholarly sources articulate the results of original research projects, or they provide expert insights concerning a theory or model. Their primary purpose is to **add to the existing body of knowledge.** The anticipated audience comprises academics, fellow researchers, and learners working toward advanced degrees. Scholarly sources are not perfect, but their policies include various processes for confirming data and mitigating partiality. For example, government sources may be able to provide very accurate statistics regarding a topic but generally will not have the capacity to provide this level of expert analysis and authentication.

> *Essentially, the work of the scholar is objective, gratuitous, a selfless act, and a by-product of the position of instructor in academia.*
>
> *~Claude Bélanger,*
> *Marianopolis College*

Determining if a source is scholarly is not a black and white science. However, there are some key features of a scholarly source. First, most scholarly sources will be peer-reviewed (also known as *refereed*) or published in a recognized scholarly publication, like a reputable journal or a college press. Peer review literally means that the article's content, review of the literature, methodology, and conclusions have been reviewed by expert scholars in that particular discipline. Peer review often involves extensive revisions to the original submission and may take up to a couple of years to actually have it published. While the standard of peer review may offer assistance in determining a scholarly source with regard to journals, it offers very little assistance towards assessing the scholarly nature of a book or Internet source.

The simplest, although not completely failsafe, way to distinguish scholarly articles is to place a checkmark in the scholarly, academic, or peer-reviewed boxes in your school's web-based library search. You also can review the journal's editorial policy. Peer review is prestigious; most journals will boast an abundance of details describing their process of peer review. The following table offers some additional helpful tips:

Scholarly Journals vs. Popular Magazines

	Scholarly Journals	Popular Magazines
Appearance	Formal and serious	Slick and glossy/ very attractive
Graphics	Graphs and Charts	Photographs and illustrations
References	Always has citations and references	May have some references but will be referenced informally
Peer Review	Evaluated by experts and only published if meets the discipline's standards	Not in the sense of scholarly peer-review
Language & Audience	Professional jargon unique to the discipline	Written for a general audience/ layperson
Intent	Inform and Report Results of Research	Provide general information to a wide audience
Advertising	No advertisement for the most part	Yes, sometimes extensive
Examples	*Crime and Delinquency* *The Leadership Quarterly*	*Popular Photography* *Time Magazine*

Books

Beware using books as sources for your papers. Some books will be acceptable to your instructor, but many will not. Obviously, anyone can write just about anything in a book. And with the advent of self-publishing, anyone can have a very attractive and scholarly looking hard cover text on the market without any credible review whatsoever. However, there are many good books, self-published or traditionally published, based on sound research and written by experts in the particular discipline. The trick is to be able to discern the acceptable from the unacceptable.

Many professors are comfortable with books published by reputable university presses such as the Harvard University Press or the Princeton University Press. While these texts may or may not be considered scholarly sources (depends on who you ask), they have met many similar measures. The authors are scholars and experts in their disciplines. The research based books have undergone significant scrutiny. Additionally, these universities take their reputation very seriously. It would be counterintuitive for them to publish anything that could jeopardize their lofty standing in academia.

There is another category of book that I accept in my courses. They are not published by university or trade presses, but they are written by experts in the field and are based on years of empirical research. *Good to Great* by Jim Collins is a good example. The book is based on years of extensive research by experts in the field. There is little evident bias; indeed, many of his findings were contrary to his, and our, existing predispositions about leadership.

Let me end this discussion on books with a comment from Dr. Stephen Verrill to one of his learners. "One noteworthy shortcoming [in your paper] is the use of a textbook citation for the source of knowledge. You must be careful citing textbooks in a discourse like this. It is okay to draw from a textbook occasionally, if there is no better source, but you want to do so sparingly. At the doctoral level, scholars read your work to get your summary and analysis of literature, not the summary and analysis of another scholar, filtered through your understanding. Before citing a textbook in scholarship, ask yourself, is this citation essential to the understanding of my argument? Is there an original source that makes the same point?"

The bottom line is that some texts will be acceptable for your papers, while others will not. If you have any concern about using a particular book, please ask your instructor.

Internet Sources

With online learning becoming so pervasive in higher education, many students, authors, and researchers now use the Internet extensively in their courses, research, and publishing. The Internet can be a tremendous source of legitimate information. Databases originating throughout the world can be accessed easily and quickly. Indeed, most students and teachers read peer-reviewed journal articles and dissertations through web-based, academic search engines such as Academic Search Premier, ERIC, and ABI/INFORM Global. Most universities offer their students and faculty access to these services free of charge. Yet, it still is virtually effortless to circulate inaccurate information and propaganda on the web also making it a tremendous source of erroneous, unreliable, unverified, and biased opinion.

My simple advice is to be cautious when using the web to find sources for your papers and assignments. Consider if the website has an identified author and if the author possesses credentials and experience that fit with the article. Consider the purpose of the website. For example, does the site promote a particular cause, which invariably will present bias? Is the website sponsored by a government agency or professional association or maybe a university with obvious peer-review mechanisms? Is the Internet article supported by appropriate citations and references? Use Internet sources wisely and judiciously and be sure to ask your instructor if you are uncertain or have any concerns about Internet sources.

Chapter

10

Plagiarism

I Get It...But, I Don't Completely Get It

Plagiarism is one of the many forms of academic dishonesty such as cheating on a test or having a fellow student or paper mill service write your paper. In a nutshell, plagiarism is the intentional, or in some cases the unintentional, use of someone's thoughts and words without giving that person credit. Plagiarism is about attribution. It is really about thievery of the mind. Most everyone gets this. We intuitively know from a young age what stealing looks like regardless of whether it is a thing or thought. We all know that copying and pasting a paragraph from the Internet into your document without proper attribution is plagiarism. Yet, plagiarism in an academic setting can be considerably more complicated.

I learned this the hard way when I was nearing the end of my doctoral course work. My professor habitually submitted all assignments to a plagiarism detection service before grading them. The report generated on my paper showed a higher than acceptable percentage score, thus appropriately setting off red flags with the professor. As I went through the highlighted sentences on the report that she provided me, I became even more confused. The service had highlighted sentences that I had paraphrased. Yes, I originally had copied and pasted the sentences but then changed a few words using the Thesaurus tool in WORD and still provided a citation. A sentence is either a quote or not, right? And obviously with changing a couple of words around here and there, the passages were not quotes. A simple citation should have been okay. Well, not so fast. The real answer rests somewhere in the middle.

Anytime you use too many of the original author's words in a string or even jumbled in the same sentence, you run the risk of plagiarism. Sometimes even a single word can be so unique that you must place quotations marks around it or risk plagiarism. Generally speaking, paraphrasing, coupled with an appropriate citation, will suffice. However, paraphrasing can be a little confusing and clearly requires some effort and critical thinking on your part.

Paraphrasing

Paraphrasing is creating a new means of expressing the original author's thoughts but in your own words. Paraphrasing is not purely reshuffling the words or just replacing words using a thesaurus. Sound paraphrasing involves dramatically transforming the original sentence with regard to verbiage and arrangement. Paraphrasing helps avoid plagiarism and assists in learning the material better because learners have to think critically about the ideas (Charleston Southern University, 2008). When learners use direct quotes, there is no requisite critical thinking of the ideas. And don't forget...even when paraphrasing, appropriate in text citations and references are required.

Referring to Other Studies

When making specific reference to someone else's material or thoughts, you also have to provide proper credit. When you point readers in the direction of a certain study, regardless of whether you discuss the thoughts or data, you need to give credit. It is very important that readers have enough information to find and read these studies for themselves if they choose. Mentioning other research studies in papers is very common in the professional literature and should be fairly common in your papers.

Self-Plagiarism

As pervasive as is the problem of learners not fully appreciating what constitutes plagiarism, imagine the problem with learners not completely understanding the concept of *self*-plagiarism. In fact, varying degrees of disagreement exist in the academic community regarding self-plagiarism. Learners may rightfully ask...How can I steal from myself? Well, the truth is you can.

Self-plagiarism, commonly referred to as *recycling fraud*, arises when writers reuse work in a new product without letting the reader know. The most blatant example of this in higher education is when a learner

> *The concept of ethical writing... entails an implicit contract between reader and writer whereby the reader assumes, unless otherwise noted, that the material was written by the author, is new, is original and is accurate to the best of the author's abilities.*
>
> ~Miguel Roig, Ph.D.

submits the same paper, or a significant portion of a paper, in multiple courses. This practice, known in the academic community as *paper recycling*, is considered plagiarism unless both professors have agreed to the multiple submissions and the practice does not violate university policy.

APA 6th Edition does allow for a very limited amount of self-duplication without attribution. When "extensive self-referencing is undesirable or awkward... and the duplicated words are limited in scope, this approach is permissible" (p. 16). The tricky part is determining what amount is considered limited in scope. APA 6th offers that writers should follow the fair use doctrine and make sure the core of the new document represents an original contribution to the field.

Common Knowledge

Thoughts, facts, and words that are commonly known may fall within the exception known as *common knowledge*. You are not required to cite and reference material is this domain. Yale College describes common knowledge as things that "...most educated people know or can find out easily in an encyclopedia or dictionary." As you can imagine from this definition, the concept and guidelines concerning common knowledge are somewhat confusing and vague and always depend on the learning community context.

Here's an example. Refer to the definition of plagiarism that I provided in the beginning of this chapter. "...plagiarism is the intentional, or in some cases the unintentional, use of someone's thoughts and words without giving that person credit." I provided no attribution for this definition although I am quite sure you could find something very similar to this in countless books and Internet sources. However, the definition I provided is commonly known within the academic community thus requiring no attribution.

Public Domain

Public domain refers to works that belong to everyone because they are not copyright protected. These works may be used as long as attribution is provided to the original author. Here's an example. "Give me liberty or give me death." Everyone reading this book knows that Patrick Henry was the original creator of this quote. You would be free to use this quote in your writings as long as you gave Patrick Henry credit, regardless of where you saw this quote while doing your research.

It still may be tough to figure out what materials are considered public domain. Here are some general rules. The copyright has expired. Generally, materials published prior to 1978 have a copyright of 75 years unless the copyright has been renewed. Generally, materials published after 1978 have a copyright length of life of the author plus 70 years (Gassaway, 2003). Additionally, federal publications are in the public domain. Lastly, some authors may not wish to have copyright protection so they freely donate their works to the public. When in doubt, always seek the publisher's permission to use the material!

Fair Use

According to the U.S. Copyright Office, one of the rights afforded to copyright owners is the exclusive privilege to "reproduce or to authorize others to reproduce their work..." One of the most important exceptions to this privilege is the standard of *fair use*. The fair use doctrine permits authors the use of copyrighted materials for a variety of purposes such as news reporting, education, academic study, and research (Newsome, 1997).

The problem with fair use is that the guidelines are vague and offer little specificity. There is no precise number of words or sentences or paragraphs that are defined within its definition. Section 107 of the U.S. copyright law establishes four factors to be considered in determining whether or not a particular use is fair. See box on next page.

Because of the imprecision of the fair use doctrine, I suggest following the U.S. Copyright Office's advice: The safest course is to obtain authorization from the copyright owner before using copyrighted material.

Factors to Be Considered in Determining *Fair Use*

---

1. The purpose and character of the use, including whether such use is of commercial nature or is for nonprofit educational purposes;

2. The nature of the copyrighted work;

3. Amount and substantiality of the portion used in relation to the copyrighted work as a whole; and

4. The effect of the use upon the potential market for or value of the copyrighted work.

Inadvertent Plagiarism

What if you honestly did not know you were committing plagiarism, yet find yourself on the wrong side of the issue? I think I have heard all the same excuses ten times. I generally do not give much credence to learners' excuses regarding work they have submitted and found to be plagiarized. But there still is a little voice in the back of my mind that sometimes wonders if learners could really be telling the truth when they proclaim they wrote the passage completely on their own, particularly if the passage is somewhat vague and within the learner's field of expertise. The root question is… *What if my thoughts aren't my thoughts at all?*

I read quite a bit. When I dive into a subject, I try to find out everything I can about it. Over the years, I have read hundreds of books and journal articles surrounding leadership. A couple of years ago, I was teaching a *What is Leadership* block at a conference. I engaged the class in a model of effective leadership that I had been developing for some time. After class, a young Air Force officer approached me. "Doc, I love your model. It's exactly what the Air Force teaches." After a demoralizing conversation, I must admit, I asked the young man to email me the Air Force model to which he was referring. He promptly did, and it was very similar to mine. As their model had been around for a long, long time, I should say mine was extremely close to theirs. So, did I plagiarize their model? Of course not... I had never seen their model, nor had I ever read anything on Air Force leadership. Yet, here my model was very similar to theirs. A cynic would say there just are not any new thoughts in this world... just ones that are remixed. I do not believe this, but I do believe that reading and studying can alter your thoughts. Indeed, this is the very purpose of higher education.

The way this usually manifests in the classroom is that a student, after being accused of plagiarism, will say that the thoughts were their own. They must have inadvertently digested some reading somewhere without consciously knowing it. This is possible as in my case with the leadership model. But in my experience, the passages that are determined to be plagiarized usually are nearly word-for-word. When this happens, the student's argument of inadvertent plagiarism really loses its steam.

My point here is to be cautious and prudent in your writings. Using someone else's words without appropriate attribution, even unintentionally from sources you have read and don't remember, still may be considered plagiarism.

Cultural Considerations

Faculty and students should be aware that not all cultures share the Western sanctity in the proprietary nature of thoughts and words. Moral and ethical values are culturally based in many contexts. The very idea that thoughts and ideas can be *stolen* is counterintuitive in some societies. I have experienced this first hand on two occasions. Several years ago, a student from another country actually submitted a photocopied article with the student's signature at the bottom. After pulling myself off the ceiling, I called the student to my office. He explained that because he had read the article, the thoughts were now his. In that he agreed with the author, there was no theft, no plagiarism. The only dilemma for me was whether to have him kicked out for plagiarism or stupidity. But seriously, not all cultures see the world in the same light as Western societies. It taught me a very important lesson. Talk about plagiarism on day one of every class, and make sure everyone understands and accepts my policies and those of the university concerning academic dishonesty.

My second experience with this phenomenon occurred when a learner from another country had a subordinate write his entire final paper. The student signed his name and submitted the paper as his own. As this learner spoke very poor English in class, and the paper was written with exceptional English grammar, the red flags went up. To make matters worse, a two day search by another faculty member determined that the paper contained substantially plagiarized material from a variety of Internet sources. If plagiarism was not such a serious offense, I would have laughed. Think about it. The subordinate was tasked to write a paper for his boss. The subordinate then plagiarized material from all over the Internet in the process. The irony was almost too much. *Okay, I did smile but no outward laughing.* When the student was interviewed, he could not understand why we were making such a big deal of this incident. He was the boss. He had rightfully ordered a subordinate to write his paper. The fact that the subordinate plagiarized materials from the Internet was not his fault; it was the subordinate's fault.

Online learning certainly makes the world smaller. It offers tremendous opportunities to bring a wealth of diversity to a single classroom. Yet, with opportunity comes challenge. It is incumbent on the university and faculty to explain plagiarism early and often in the graduate program as all students will be held accountable under the same rules and policies.

How Do My Professors Know?

Most universities have stringent policies against academic dishonesty. They preach these policies starting with the very first course. Yet, plagiarism remains at epidemic levels.

Sadly, professors see plagiarism on a monthly, weekly, sometimes even daily basis. Yet, there is no doubt professors miss many plagiarism cases through inattention, lack of knowledge in the field, or more probably, the student just got one by them. I know I do not have time to carefully

> *... almost 80% of undergraduate student respondents reported one or more incidents of cheating.*
>
> ~*Donald L. McCabe*
> *Center for Academic Integrity*

scrutinize every discussion posting throughout the day. Just reading every posting and providing substantive responses take tremendous effort and time. Having said this, the ability to detect plagiarism has exponentially increased with the advent of Internet services that sniff out millions of documents looking for similar strings of words. These services are not perfect, but they do have their rightful place in higher education.

Even with the exponential growth in the use of these Internet services, professors primarily still catch plagiarism using old fashioned, tried and true strategies. It is all about red flags. First, most professors teach subjects they have spent years studying and researching. They know the literature. They know what the well-known authors say. They even know the tone many of these authors use. When professors see something specifically familiar in a paper, it sets off red flags.

Professors also know the tone and styles of their students. Particularly in an online environment, within a couple of weeks I pretty much can identify my learners by just reading their postings. When instructors see a change in style, when they see a change in grammar or APA, when they see inconsistency in any way, red flags go up.

Sometimes, students blatantly raise the red flag. Occasionally, I have papers submitted that have no citations yet refer to theories and models well beyond common knowledge. Obviously, this almost always represents part ignorance and part plagiarism. On several occasions, I was grading papers when the font suddenly changed from Times New Roman to Arial or some other font...then back again after a couple of paragraphs. Well, you don't have to be a rocket scientist to figure out this one. I submit papers like this to the Mydropbox plagiarism detection service, and within minutes, I generally have a report in my hand with abundant evidence of plagiarism. Many times the paragraphs are word-for-word copied and pasted with no citation whatsoever.

There are numerous ways that instructors detect plagiarism. However, I can assure you that most faculty members detest having to be the plagiarism police! Do your work ethically and simply do not put them in the position to have to scrutinize your assignments for evidence of plagiarism.

Consequences of Plagiarism

Plagiarism is serious. The ramifications for the violating student are harsh. However, the costs to the scientific research community may be more significant than the individual implications of plagiarism. Research, whether in the physical or social sciences, implies trust. Trust that the material is original and adding to the body of knowledge. Trust that the data was collected ethically and with sound methodology. Trust that the results were not unduly biased. Plagiarism represents a blatant violation of this trust. As Al-Awqati (2007) observed, "It is first and foremost a breach of faith in the social contract between reader and writer."

There are many individual consequences surrounding plagiarism. Even in instances where the student and instructor worked out the issue through resubmission of the paper or some other similar remedy, the student's work for the duration of the course will receive tremendous scrutiny that may otherwise not have occurred.

Generally, students who plagiarize will, at minimum, fail that specific assignment. As you can imagine, getting a zero on a major paper presents a significant challenge in passing the overall course. Students also may be assigned a failing grade for the

> *The penalties for plagiarism can be surprisingly severe, ranging from failure of classes and expulsion from academic institutions to heavy fines and jail time!*
>
> *Plagiarism.org*

entire course or in some instances be dismissed from the university.

Glicken (2003) discussed a situation in which a degree was rescinded and the transcript was changed to indicate that the learner was expelled for cheating. You also may be familiar with the well-known University of Virginia case. As a result of suspected plagiarism in his classes, Professor Bloomfield created a computer program designed to identify resemblances in papers. Several learners eventually had their diplomas rescinded by the university (Thompson, 2006).

Finally, plagiarism may have legal consequences as it may infringe upon the copyrighted intellectual work of others thus violating copyright laws. And authors do not necessarily have to register a copyright in order for the material to have copyrighted status. Materials created since 1978 are copyright protected from the minute the work takes a concrete form, regardless of whether or not the material has official copyright status with the U.S. Copyright Office. A general rule of thumb in the publishing community is that writers can borrow, with attribution of course, small portions (less than 500 words) of published work (APA, 2001). Yet, this is only a guide and does not necessarily overcome copyright issues.

Here is an example. Look at the poem I borrowed from Sean Covey and placed in Part III. The word count is minimal, and I gave him credit for the poem. However, the material is copyrighted with a clear message to all prohibiting the use of this material without the publisher's permission. Thus, I asked for and received permission from Sean Covey and the publisher to include his poem in this book.

The penalties for copyright infringement are potentially very harsh. It could mean a criminal conviction because violating copyright law is a federal crime. It could mean having to defend yourself in a civil suit. While *fair use* standards generally protect learners, the guidelines are somewhat vague and confusing. The message here is to be particularly careful when considering using copyrighted materials. When in doubt, always seek permission from the publisher.

Avoiding Plagiarism

Some learners seem to think that adding citations hurts the credibility of their papers. New graduate learners may believe that the paper will be devalued because the professor was looking only for the learner's original thoughts. This is an honest mistake learners may make, but nevertheless, it is a mistake. Unless you are writing an opinion paper or specifically told otherwise by your instructors, they are not looking solely for your original thoughts. They want you to research the literature, analyze what you have found, apply critical thinking skills through synthesis and evaluation. Citing good sources actually adds credibility to your paper as it gives the indication (and evidence) that you have done your homework and are beginning to learn the relevant literature in that discipline. Plagiarism largely may be avoided by keeping a few things in mind.

Tips for Avoiding Plagiarism

1. Avoid taking the easy way by out by copying and pasting. Most of us know right from wrong. Just do the right thing.

2. Provide accurate in text citations and corresponding references for other authors' thoughts.

3. Use quotation marks when directly quoting and provide a page number in the citation.

4. Check every citation against every reference and accordingly, every reference against every citation.

5. Study your style manual often! Sometimes a vague area will arrise between plagiarism and improper citing and referencing. The style manual can help alleviate this ambiguity.

6. Do not even consider using *paper mills* that write papers for you. Trust me, your teachers will spot this a mile away. Not to mention, most of the papers coming out of these mills are old and dated.

7. Consider using an Internet based plagiarism detection service. While services like these are used by faculty to deter and detect plagiarism, possibly their greatest benefit is their ability to teach.

Final Thoughts

Obviously, plagiarism is wrong. It is stealing. Indeed, many would argue that intellectual theft is a greater moral offense than proper theft. But beyond the morality of the issue is the inherent learning problem with plagiarism. *Learning* is absent in plagiarized work. "Reputations in academia are made on the basis of creating new knowledge: discoveries of new facts, new ways of looking at previously known facts, original analysis of old ideas" (Standler, 2000). The absence of critical thinking and analysis negates the very purpose of higher education.

Chapter

11

Strategies
for
Success

Knowing the *lay of the land* will help you succeed in any endeavor. Indeed, understanding the nuances, traps, and insider knowledge is a key to any successful endeavor. The one theme I consistently hear when talking with graduates of traditional and online programs is, "I wish I knew then what I know now." Chapter 11 is designed for this very purpose - to offer simple, candid strategies for success in the courseroom.

Know Yourself

Before jumping into your first class, spend a little time on some honest self-assessment. No one is great at everything. In fact, most of us are really good at some things and equally bad at others. I know, for example, that organizational skills are not among my natural talents. I do a pretty good job with those tasks because I continuously force myself to go beyond my comfort zone, but I doubt that I ever

> *If you know others and know yourself, you need not fear the result of a hundred battles;*
>
> *If you know yourself but not others, for every victory, you will also suffer a defeat;*
>
> *If you know neither yourself nor others, you will succumb in every battle.*
>
> ~*Sun Tzu*

will be great at those skills. The associated strength, however, is that I'm comfortable in times of crisis, and I enjoy having to think quickly on my feet. While these strengths were beneficial in graduate school, my weaknesses could have been fatal flaws without self-awareness and perseverance to overcome them. Poor organizational skills will doom a graduate student. If you naturally do not possess these skills, you need to learn them. Organizational skills are just one example. The point is to honestly assess what you are bringing to the program and the skills you need to further hone.

Rigor and Balance

Know that some classes will be easier than others, and conversely, some will be so demanding as to make you question your intellectual capacity, reasons for starting a graduate program, and even your sanity. This may be a result of the curriculum design, or it may be just a difference in the personalities and paradigms of different instructors. Regardless, just know that when things are running a little too good to be true, it won't last. And also as true, just when you think you are at your wits end with the world crumbling around you, this too shall pass.

I vividly recall going strong through my first couple of doctoral classes. Straight As on assignments with glowing remarks. "You're such an asset to this program," and "Your writing skills are outstanding." Then, in about course number three, I received, "Your writing is at the master's level at best. Your attention to scholarly writing, scholarly sources, and Bloom's Taxonomy is weak. Let's talk." After drying off from that cold bucket of fresh reality, we did talk, and I began to get serious about my critical thinking skills and writing. The duration of my coursework was similar to these first three classes. Some were less demanding; others were brutally difficult. That's just life, and you will do much better with this perspective in mind as you traverse your academic adventure.

Alignment

Graduate school is tough enough, particularly if you are not enjoying yourself or getting a sense of relevant value from your hard work. So, why not align your courses with your work or personal interests? You can do this in many ways, although there are two strategies sure to work for just about everyone. First, every program has a cadre of electives with which you can choose a variety of courses usually even from other schools and disciplines within your university. Pick something fun or interesting to you. Choose a class that fills a particular gap you see missing from your program. Pick a course that has direct relevance to something going on in your life or at work... maybe an organizational change class. Select a course that you feel would look good on a resume or to your employer. The primary reason programs have electives is to offer students flexibility to customize their degrees to some level and round out gaps and areas of interest. Don't miss out on this opportunity.

The second way you can align your courses is to massage the assignments, particularly the larger final projects, around an area of interest. Many projects and assignments have specific parameters, but many others afford learners the opportunity to explore their particular contexts of choice. Take this opportunity. It will make the program seem so much more relevant and personal, and may even provide you with something tangible you can use at work or home.

Thinking Ahead

Many professors will advise you during your course work, as well as during your residencies, that the surest way to graduation is to take everything one step at a time. "Don't get ahead of yourself," I heard so many times. Without a doubt, you do have to focus on the now before looking to future. We see it all the time in football. The quarterback throws a perfect pass. The receiver extends and right as the ball touches his hands, the receiver turns and runs, without actually catching the ball, and yes...Incomplete pass!

HOWEVER, students who never look ahead, who never plan for the future, are the students who will have ABD (All But Dissertation) beside their name instead of Ph.D. Stay in the minute, stay focused, but keep a squinted eye on the future. Let me give you a couple of examples.

> *He who fails to plan,*
> *plans to fail.*
> *Proverb*

Start thinking about a dissertation topic sooner rather than later. Now would be a good time. Picking a realistic topic takes time and commitment and usually a significant amount of collaboration among you, your peers, professors, and mentor. Dissertation topics and research questions usually start out very broad in nature and have to be narrowed down repeatedly. The sooner you start thinking about a general topic, the more prepared you will be as the dissertation phase gets closer.

Another benefit of choosing a topic earlier in your course work is that you can start developing a level of expertise in that field with regard to the existing literature. I knew early in my doctoral program that I wanted to do something regarding the relationship between personality and leadership. So, I took the opportunity in my courses to write papers in the field of leadership and personality. For example, in the Human Development course, I wrote my final paper on personality development. I fulfilled my final course project with a relevant paper, AND I started building my knowledge base <u>and</u> reference base. These references came in very handy as I progressed through the comprehensive exam into the dissertation stage and began working on the literature review chapter of my dissertation.

Course Mechanics

Okay, you've found a few minutes of quiet time to focus on school. It is a new week with new discussion questions and assignments. You log-in to the course. Consider going through the following checklist before getting to the heart of the week. Check your courseroom mail first. With many online programs, this is the primary venue of private communication you will have with you instructor and peers. Of course, there always is the exception. In my classes, I do not use the courseroom email. Before the start of each course, I set up a new category in the discussion room called Private Discussions. I do this for each learner as a separate topic. When students need to converse with me privately, they simply post to this private area. Only the learner and I can see the post. I do this for several reasons, but the benefit to the students is that it is one less place they have to check when logging into the class.

Next, check the assignment area. You may have a graded paper waiting for you. More importantly, you may have a returned paper waiting for you that has no grade. Very often, I send papers back the first time for students to re-work before assigning the paper a grade. Most students respond to me fairly quickly. However, in every class, I have a couple of students who do not know the paper is even there because they don't check the assignment area until the next assignment is due, which could be weeks ahead.

Lastly, go the discussion area of the courseroom. This is where the course really comes alive with peer and faculty engagement. And yes, this is where my Private Discussion category is set up for personal communications.

Before focusing on the discussion questions and assignments for that particular unit or week, take a look at four very important areas. The first is the Updates and Handouts section. Faculty often post things of interest or need in there. For example, generally in week one, I will post the Common APA and Writing checklist that I included in this book. The second important area to view is the Ask Your Instructor thread. Regardless of whether or not you are the one who asked the question, you will benefit by reading every single posting in this thread. I always ask students to ask me personal questions that are specific to them by way of the Private Discussions area. However, I ask that they use the Ask Your Instructor thread to ask questions that probably will pertain to everyone. Finally, look in the Cyber Café area. Different schools call it different things, but this is the thread designed solely for students. It's a thread where you can ask peers questions or talk about things that are a little off topic. Instructors rarely go in this thread, so please don't ask us questions in there. I say *rarely* because instructors will check the thread occasionally just to make sure the content and tone is civil and professional. While this is your thread, it's still not an anything goes area.

Okay, you've spent a brief few minutes going through the daily log-in mechanics. Now, it is time to dive into the week's readings, discussions, and assignments. Get out of the discussion area and go to the Learning Units section and then click on the unit of the week. Read and print the introduction as well as the readings, assignment(s) and discussion questions. This also is a good time to view any multi-media pieces that may be embedded in the unit. Once you have completed the readings and multi-media associated with the discussion questions, you are ready to write your initial postings.

Discussion Postings

Prepare your discussion questions in WORD. It makes life so much easier. It is much simpler to check your spelling, and you will have a permanent record of all your work. I suggest creating a folder at the beginning of each course. Within that folder, you can create sub-folders for every unit that will serve as files for all of the discussion postings, assignments, and references. This will come in handy as you progress to the comps and even the dissertation! Copy your post from the WORD document and paste it into the courseroom discussion thread.

Keep a few things in mind when posting. All professors will require you to be civil and respectful, but the unanimity stops there. Different instructors have different views on the management of the discussions. For example, some instructors like to maintain a high level of formality in the courseroom. Postings should be in APA format and follow normal rules of grammar such as no contractions. Postings should be supported by peer-reviewed sources. Other instructors like to keep the discussion area more informal, relaxed, and colloquial. I like to think I strike a balance, as do most faculty members. I require that assignments be prepared with academic standards and formality, but I like to keep the courseroom discussions relaxed. My humble view is that assignments are meant to provide the learner an opportunity to learn theory and practice scholarly writing, while the mission of the discussion threads is to bring context and applicability to those theories in a more colloquial environment. The point here is to give your instructors what they want. It's college 101. Saying that Dr. Smith handled things this way or that way will carry zero weight with Dr. Jones. Give them want they ask.

You also will be required to post responses to other learners' initial postings. These postings have to be substantive and should poke, pry, instigate a little, and perhaps make the learner think a little deeper. Most instructors will agree that a little disagreement is a good thing in the courseroom. What your responses to fellow learners should not do is create undue busy work for your peers in an attempt to look good to the teacher or show how intelligent you are to the rest of the class. Everyone is swamped in a graduate program.

Engage and poke and pry but don't gratuitously pile on more work for your colleagues by asking unrelated or superfluous questions. Bottom line with your postings is to keep them substantive, civil, and yes, even a little spirited.

Assignments

Many of the same issues with discussion postings apply to assignments, but I want to mention just a couple of tips. First, always attach your documents to the assignment area as opposed to typing directly into that area. It often is very hard to read the assignment if not attached, and there is no way to assess and offer constructive criticism regarding APA issues.

Secondly, read and re-read the assignment directions. Quite often I get nicely prepared submissions clearly at the graduate level, yet the student did not follow the directions. Sometimes the submissions answer great questions but not the questions posed in the assignment. Please take the time to read and digest what the assignment really entails. This attention to detail will become critical in the comprehensive exam phase.

> *Assignments are like bills; it only takes being behind on a couple for it to start weighing on even the most diligent of us – it just keeps mounting and mounting, until it is an unscalable mountain of work.*
>
> Rebecca Brown
> Author
> *The Secret to Online Success*

Timeliness

As with any endeavor in any higher education program, some instructors are lenient with deadlines, and some are real sticklers. Many teachers start deducting points the day after the assignment or posting is due, and I have known some who simply will not accept late assignments. These decisions are not arbitrarily made by instructors out of rigidity and strict adherence to rules. It is done to keep learners engaged and on track. My experience has been that once learners start turning in late assignments or asking for extensions, they never fully recover. Similarly, I have only once in years of teaching granted an Incomplete grade to a learner at the end of the course, and that learner actually complete the course work the next semester. The incompletes almost always turn to Fs. It is a slippery slope you do not want to start down. Read the Faculty Expectations carefully to get a sense for what your individual instructor's tolerance levels is regarding timely submissions. If you have emergencies and problems, reach out to your instructors before the due date. You may be surprised how understanding they can be. Yet, as a rule, find a way to get your homework completed on time!

The whole issue of timeliness goes back to organization, planning, and time management skills that Dr. Noah discussed in Chapter 7. Procrastination simply is a luxury that will not be tolerated in graduate school. Timeliness also speaks to the broader characteristics of commitment and dedication to the program. It speaks to fairness and equality among students as well. As busy as you are, most of your fellow learners are just as busy. Get your work in on time. But Doc, how do I get all the assignments, discussions, and that voluminous amount of reading done in one week?

Skim and Go

I mentioned in the introduction to Part III my first experience with doctoral level work at Temple University. If you recall, another student and I were having a hard time understanding how a human being could read 500 to 1,000 pages a week and do all the associated assignments. My professor counseled, "Gentlemen, first let me explain doctoral level reading. Ph.D.s read for patterns and themes. They skim and learn to hone in on what's important and avoid what's not." A few weeks ago, I had this same conversation with a colleague at work. I gave him the similar response I had been given years ago. He said, "Oh, you mean like *Skim and Go*." Yes, that is exactly what I mean.

Academic reading requires a different approach than reading for pleasure. Read the abstract of the articles, the introduction, and the discussion. Then skim through the methodology, statistics, and literature review. You can cover a lot of material this way. When you get to a journal article that looks very promising for your specific needs, then you can spend more time with the details. When reading a book, you can try the same strategy. Read the preface, the introduction, and take a hard look at the contents page. Then hone in on the particular area germane to the assignment or discussion.

Graduate school, particularly in the online environment, is all about reading and writing. You have to train yourself with study habits that are probably very different from when you earned your undergraduate degree. Successful grad students learn skim and go reading. They learn to look for patterns and areas with a specific nexus to their assignments, and they learn to hone in for a serious read on the topics that are more complex and relevant to their needs.

Study Habits

Students have to find their own way with regard to developing individual study habits. Some need several hours at a time of strict peace and quiet. While this would be ideal, it generally did not happen that way for me. I did take those long study times once or twice a week, but my overall style was to take every little 15 minute chance I could find to complete my readings, answer discussion questions, respond to peers, and work on assignments. My motive was to take as little time away from my family as possible. So I planned my little breaks around their activities. When I did have to have those several hours at a time blocks, which was frequently, I generally would work late at night after everyone was asleep. I didn't get much sleep for a few years, but as I have said over and over, graduate school is about sacrifice. Something had to give, and I chose that something to be sleep as opposed to missing the kids' soccer and lacrosse games.

Final Thoughts

Completing your course work is a huge milestone. Make sure to recognize not only the big milestones but also the smaller accomplishments. My wife and I celebrated with a "date" after every quarter…just the two of us…dinner, movie, whatever. I remember saying things like, "2 down, 10 to go…4 down, 8 to go." Before I knew it, I was approaching the comprehensive exam!

Another way to celebrate your successes is to do it in a face-to-face environment with other learners and faculty. Such an environment creates opportunities to share experiences, strategies for success, and yes, celebrate your accomplishments with people who understand. While not all programs have such a residency requirement, many do. Those that do often refer to this as the *Colloquium*.

Part
IV

It's Face-to-Face Time

Traversing the Colloquium

*If the courseroom is the heart of an online education,
the colloquium is her soul.*

Chapter 12

What is a *Colloquium?*

Col·lo·qui·um   (kə-lō′kwē-əm)   n.   *pl.* **col·lo·qui·a** (-kwē-ə)

From Latin *colloquy*, conversation.

1. An informal meeting for the exchange of views.
2. A conference at which scholars or other experts present papers, analyze, and discuss a specific topic.

Now that you know the origin and definition of the word, let me tell you what it *really* means. The colloquium is a residential requirement at some online universities for certain Master's and Doctoral degrees. Many online universities and traditional universities with online programs have residency requirements created to fit their unique contexts. Some are a few days over a long weekend like Capella's new model while others may last upwards of a week. Walden University, for example, requires 20 days of residency overall in their doctoral programs (two 4-day and two 6-day events).

Doctoral colloquia generally are designed to address the four Ph.D. competencies of critical thinking, research, scholarly communication, and the scholar-practitioner model. Learners are required to attend classes and engage in a variety of workshops to hone these competencies. While these educational outcomes are very important, the overarching benefits of the colloquium experience are to share common experiences and strengthen the sense of community among learners and faculty. Some residency programs offer a Distinguished Speaker Series in which well-known leaders and figures in a variety of contexts address learners collectively in large plenary sessions. These speakers truly provide real-world context and insights to the issues important to learners. As Capella University observes, "At colloquia, you'll interact with faculty and your peers on a new level. You'll put courseroom theory into practice, connecting on a personal and scholarly basis. You'll learn from and inspire each other, participating in small and large academic sessions, clinical skills labs, and panel discussions...You'll collaborate and build a strong learning community—a factor that can help strengthen and maintain motivation so that you'll continue moving toward your degree." Colloquia really do provide a venue for learners to meet peers, advisors, and faculty in a face-to-face, secure, stimulating, and supportive environment.

> *I really felt an overwhelming excitement when I attended my first colloquium. For the first time, it all felt real. I felt like a part of something tangible. The university became something I actually could reach out and touch.*
>
> *Tara Smallwood*
> *Ph.D. learner*
> *Capella University*
> *Class of 2009*

Here's how Capella handles their colloquia., which is fairly similar to other residency programs. Doctoral learners attend each of the three tracks at specific times during their course work depending on where they are in the program. Online prerequisite activities accompany each track in an effort to make the most of the residency experience in the most efficient time.

Track 1 learners attend in the beginning of their course work and are exposed to orientation workshops, policies, best practices, and an assortment of resources such as the mobile writing center, career services, computer lab, and library services. One of the special aspects of Track 1 is the cohort setting in which learners meet with the same faculty member and small group of peers each morning to discuss anything and everything concerning their colloquium experience and overall program. I have spent mornings discussing academic writing, APA, and scholarly sources with learners. I also have spent mornings briefly touching upon the comprehensive exam and dissertation although faculty do try to keep Track 1 learners focused on their course work. I always am amazed at the degree these same learners stay in touch and help each other through their entire degree program.

Track 2 generally is taken about mid-way through a learner's course work phase. This track emphasizes issues more specific to a learner's particular field of study. For example, Track 1 may have workshops identifying new knowledge bases and academic skill sets while the Track 2 experience engages learners in applying new knowledge with regard to critical thinking and problem solving in their particular discipline. General topics that are very germane to learner success also will be discussed such as statistics, SPSS, and research ethics.

Track 3 has similar substantive classes in various disciplines but really begins to focus learners on the comprehensive examination and dissertation. Substantive workshops honing writing skills and critical thinking are offered as well as procedural seminars attempting the answer the *how to* questions learners naturally have. Track 3 even has seminars discussing post graduation interests such as how to write a vitae, understanding hierarchy in higher education, and how to find a job as a full-time or adjunct instructor. Many learners even walk away from Track 3 with a specific, workable dissertation topic and research questions to guide the dissertation.

Beyond the social events planned nearly every evening, my favorite part of the colloquium experience were (and still are) the special sessions. Consistent with the colloquium theme of identifying with your particular field or profession, many schools offer informal sessions concerning your specialization. For example, the School of Public Safety Leadership may host a seminar over lunch on the topic of Criminal Justice or Emergency Management. This allows learners and faculty in those fields the opportunity to discuss trends and practices in a relaxed and informal setting. Alumni panels are another example of special learning sessions that involve inviting several alumni to speak about their experiences as an online learner and graduate. The question and answer component is both lively and informational. What a great experience for learners and alumni!

Final Thoughts

The colloquium experience offers learners unparalleled opportunities to critically discuss issues among scholars, meet new people, and truly develop an incredible sense of community among learners, staff, and faculty. You will do just fine with no guidance from me, but there are a few tips that are sure to enhance your experience.

> *The excitement and anticipation that learners bring to the colloquium is impressive and reflects deeply held commitments to achieve doctoral education goals.*
>
> Pamela Patrick, Ph.D.
> Capella University
> Academic Director of
> Colloquium

114

Chapter 13

Strategies for Success

*The results you achieve will be in direct proportion
to the effort you apply.*

Walt Disney

The colloquium experience, as with all of life's endeavors, is what you make it. Before we look at any specific strategies, start thinking about your willingness to engage, participate, and have an open mind. Your attendance is required during the colloquium, but there are no tests, no grades – it is what you make it. You can walk away with some useful, basic information or end the colloquium with a treasure trove of new knowledge, practices, and an entire network of friends and colleagues. It's your call.

Preparing for Colloquium

Assuming you already have registered for the colloquium, preparation should begin with reading *About Colloquium*. Pay particular attention to little things such as what to bring, what to wear, various expenses, and lodging. Make reservations early as these sites tend to fill quickly, and you find yourself having to stay a mile down the road at another hotel. Not the end of the world but not the most optimal either. You may want to think about transportation too. Although, most colloquia tend to be fairly self-contained, some learners will want a rental car. Most learners (and faculty) pay scant attention to transportation beyond to and from the airport.

The next preparatory item on your calendar should be to consider if you have special needs. Persons with some disabilities, for example, may have mobility needs that should be addressed before arriving. Your university will be fully committed to making the colloquium a positive experience for everyone – just give them a heads up a couple of weeks out.

Next, read the colloquium schedule if your university publishes one before the event. The schedule may have a list of faculty who will be attending from each school as well as an agenda of all academic sessions and workshops. Get your thoughts together and start scratching out a draft schedule of what you want to attend. The great thing about colloquia is that multiple workshops are available at the same time, so you are afforded a significant level of freedom in customizing the colloquium to your unique needs. Once you are satisfied with your schedule, open your day planner and write it all in. Make sure to schedule some one-on-one time with your advisor or favorite faculty members. This is a great time, particularly in later tracks, to start thinking about dissertation committees and to start developing a dissertation topic. One last thing – print the handouts for each session you plan on attending. Many colloquia workshops require that you bring the handouts. Typically, there are on-site printing stations that can accommodate reasonable printing needs.

Because you do not need to register for individual classes ahead of time, you will not be held to your planned schedule. But having a tentative idea before you get to the colloquium of what you want to accomplish is an empowering way to limit stress, stay organized, and get the most from the entire experience.

Finally, make sure to complete any prerequisite work such as online courses, discussions, or modules. Some universities will still allow you to attend the event without the prerequisite work completed, but the experience will not be as rich as if you had completed the work.

Day One

Check in the hotel, take your bags to your room, and then register with the university folks. Checking in with the university (signing your name) is very important. Just as important, please do not leave the colloquium on the last day without signing out. Sign-out procedures are explained in the colloquium planner as well as in the school opening meeting and cohort meetings. Following the sign-in and sign-out procedures ensure that you receive credit for attending the colloquium!

Next, I suggest getting a lay of the land - maybe an hour long walk just to absorb my surroundings. I suggest stopping by the bookstore, check out where the major meeting rooms are located, and look for any last minute changes or additions to the schedule. I even take time to walk around outside before the colloquium officially kicks off. I remember my Track 3 colloquium in Jacksonville, Florida. The colloquium was in a beautiful hotel right on the river. What a perfect start to the week by walking the river bank and taking in a little of what that great town had to offer.

The next step is to attend your school specific welcome. You probably can get away without going as far as credit for attendance, but don't rob yourself of this experience. It doesn't last too long, and it provides an invigorating and motivational context for the entire week. This also is a great opportunity to start meeting new peers and faculty.

Don't Be an Island

While online learning offers tremendous benefits, as we discussed in the opening chapters of this book, it can leave students feeling a little out of sorts, particularly in their first quarter. The colloquium experience, with encouragement from the staff, faculty, and other students, helps learners begin to develop more confidence in their capacity to work at the graduate or doctoral level.

> *Do not ever sit by yourself! If you don't know anyone in the session, make sure to sit at a table with people already there, introduce yourself, then sit back, listen, learn, and be a contributing member of the group.*
>
> Kevin Kupietz
> Ph.D. learner
> Capella University
> Class of 2010

The colloquium experience offers occasions for learners, staff, and faculty to interact with each other. Through workshops and sessions or more informal social events and meals, students will have a variety of opportunities to engage each other and faculty in scholarly discussions, share common experiences, and expand their network of peers. But if you want to be shy, stubborn, or anything less than engaging, you probably will be able to get away with it. Of course, you only would be hurting yourself. Get out of your comfort zone. Trust that your peers and faculty will support you. Network, liaison, and don't be an island unto yourself!

Proactive Learning

Savvy learners take advantage of the many services at colloquia beyond scheduled sessions and workshops. These opportunities may include library and research services, the Career Center, doctoral advising, and a mobile writing center. A colleague I work with was having problems in his first couple of classes transitioning to scholarly, academic writing. He spent every free minute during Track 1 hanging out in the writing lab, and he even scheduled a one-on-one session with a writing professional. He said better writing was the number one tangible take-away from his first colloquium experience.

It's Over – Now What?

Have no fear about the continuing support of the university. All of the services at colloquia are within reach throughout your degree. Yet, there are a few things you should do over the first few weeks after you have completed a colloquium.

Take a few minutes to reflect on the experience. It sounds a little abstract, but it is a worthwhile endeavor. Ask yourself what you gained from the colloquium, and what you want from your next residency. Ask yourself what you could have done differently to better prepare before the colloquium, and what you could have done during the colloquium to better exploit the experience. Most importantly, identify what behaviors you will change now that you are equipped with a whole new set of skills, knowledge, and friends.

This is a good time to solidify the relationships you established in the colloquium. Undoubtedly, you exchanged emails and phone numbers with a variety of peers and faculty. Don't wait until the next residency to speak to these folks. Take time to drop them a quick hello in the following days after a colloquium, and then stay in touch with them periodically. Honestly, I don't know what I would have done without the constant wisdom of two peers going through similar doctoral programs with me: Dr. Tim Turner, University of Virginia, and Dr. Jim Ford, Capella University. You really will need a strong support base at various milestones and tough spots throughout the program. Your family will represent your biggest fan base and certainly will rejoice with you in your accomplishments. Yet, who better to help you through the various obstacles and savor the successes of different milestones than a peer group who truly gets what you are going through? Develop a strong network of peers and stay engaged with them.

Part
V

The Ultimate Test

Passing the Comprehensive Exam

You know from past experiences that whenever you have been driven to the wall, or thought you were, you have extricated yourself in a way which you never would have dreamed possible had you not been put to the test. The trouble is that in your everyday life you don't go deep enough to tap the divine mind within you.

Orson Welles

It is important to recognize that comprehensive exams (sometimes referred to as qualifying exams) come in many shapes, sizes, and formats. The requirements and administration of them are as varied as the universities and programs of which they are housed. While Part V provides a brief overview of the main three categories of comprehensive exams, it is beyond the scope of this text to offer specific guidance concerning every derivation of the exam. The intention of Part V is to offer guidance and strategies that may assist all learners pass the comps. However, at various times, particularly in Chapter 16, the context will narrow to the comps process at Capella University.

Chapter

14

Do We Really Need a Test Here?

The comprehensive exam (a.k.a. "the comps") is an integral component towards to the completion of the doctoral degree as well as many master's degrees in both traditional and web-based universities. Every college and program administers the comps differently, but all adhere to a consistent theme. The overarching purpose of the comprehensive exam is to test learners' knowledge in their particular discipline, assess critical thinking skills, and determine their ability to communicate at the appropriate scholarly level. Comprehensive exams generally focus on application, methodology, and theory.

Throughout the course work, individual instructors served as both the teacher and assessor. The comprehensive exam phase is the first real occasion in the program where the university stands up as a *collective* and says, "Okay, good grades and perseverant, but can we trust that the learner is capable of conducting original research in a competent and ethical manner and then communicating the conclusions in a scholarly fashion?" It is imperative at this juncture that the university determines if learners have sufficiently progressed toward the role of scholar-practitioner, expanded an expertise in their discipline, and established a foundation as a scholarly communicator with regard to both written and oral presentation.

Most comprehensive exams are either pass or fail, and many programs require students to support their responses in an *oral defense* in which faculty committee members dig deeper into the student's knowledge and insights about their responses. My doctoral comps oral defense lasted nearly two hours and was one of the most rigorous endeavors I ever have experienced.

Methods of Delivery

While many derivations of administering the comps exist, there are three overarching formats I believe to be the most prevalent. The first method is the requirement for learners to complete several exams (papers) during their course work regarding discipline related topics. There is no distinct comprehensive exam phase in this situation.

The second method requires students to show up at a test site in the morning and write for several hours typically having to answer three or four questions. Students will not know what the questions will be but will have a sense of the broader topic areas such as statistics, research methodology, research ethics, or any number of discipline related topics. Students typically will have been supplied a reading list well in advance. In fact, I received the comps reading list during my master's program in my very first class! And yes, it was very lengthy comprising hundreds of books and journal articles. Upon completion of the exam, students photocopy their papers, give the originals to the comps administrator, and spend the next couple of days typing their responses directly from the photocopy. Final typed papers are then submitted to accompany the original submission for grading.

The final method is a version of the take home exam philosophy. Once students complete their required course work, they move into the comprehensive exam phase. Students are assigned a mentor (comps committee chair) during this process. When learners are ready to begin the exam, they notify their courseroom mentor at which time the learners are provided comprehensive exam questions... generally three or four questions depending on the university. The learner then has a specified period to complete the papers all within a specified number of pages. A typical situation would be four weeks to prepare three doctoral level responses not to exceed 50 pages.

All But Dissertation (ABD)

Passing the comprehensive exam is a significant milestone in the journey towards earning your doctorate. It also confers a certain status often referred to as ABD or more preferably, doctoral candidate. I think it is worthwhile to mention the concept of ABD because professors and mentors receive so many questions about this topic.

Technically, ABD refers to the status of a student upon completing the course work and comprehensive exam. You may have seen someone's name with the initials ABD after it. However, for two reasons, I recommend you avoid adding these letters after your name. The first reason is that the ABD designation is becoming dated and irrelevant. Several times of late, I have seen "Ph.D.(c)" beside a person's name. Not knowing what this meant, I eventually did some digging. The (c) stands for candidate. In other words, this designation means the same as the ABD designation. Personally, I have ethical concerns with this because the average person will not know what the (c) means, and they will incorrectly assume the person has a Ph.D.

The second reason not to use the designation is the message it sends. When I see ABD, I see someone who made it through the course work and comprehensive exam but did not have the fortitude to bring it home with the dissertation. Frankly, when I see ABD beside someone's name, I immediately think quitter. This, of course,

> *Being ABD is a wonderful thing... as long as it doesn't last too long!*
>
> *Julia Moore, Ph.D.*
> *Comprehensive Exam Mentor*
> *Capella University*

is a brutal assessment often not based in the reality of the situation. Yet, human nature is a force to be reckoned with, and this immediate judgment is shared among many scholars and academics. Of course, many good people never make it past the ABD status because of legitimate issues like finances, health problems, family concerns, and so forth. So, clearly it is not fair to paint a broad brush over all ABD learners. Additionally, some students who have been in the ABD status just a short time will want to take advantage of this designation if they are applying to job positions in academe before graduation. My suggestion is to explain your status rather than using acronyms by your name. It will serve you better to say that you have completed your course work and comprehensive exam and are working on your dissertation, as opposed to simply placing these three letters beside your name.

Final Thoughts

The comprehensive exam is necessary for you and the university. It serves as a measure for the university to assess your readiness for the dissertation, and it represents a growth opportunity for learners through extensive reading, review of the literature, and scholarly writing. The following chapter speaks directly to the appropriate critical thinking skills needed in the comprehensive exam phase.

Chapter

15

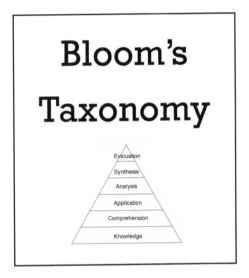

Bloom's

Taxonomy

As learners begin completing their first courses, a change starts to occur with regard to the way they digest information and make sense of all the new knowledge they are gaining. Students progress through various stages beginning with memorization and culminating with the capacity to evaluate existing theories and models and create new ways of thinking. This evolution can, in some measure, be described through the analysis and application of the Taxonomy of Educational Objectives, commonly referred to as Bloom's Taxonomy (1956).

The Concept

In 1956, Benjamin Bloom led an endeavor with a group of psychologists and scholars to formulate a way of classifying learning objectives and educational activities. The classifications provide faculty with a structure that may be used to establish curriculum and programs that enable students to think more critically as they progress in their studies. Three domains were identified: Cognitive, affective, and psychomotor.

The affective domain describes learners' reactive emotional responses. The psychomotor domain refers to learner's capacity to change their behavior as part of the learning process. The cognitive domain encompasses critical thinking and problem solving skills (Krathwohl, 2002). While the affective and psychomotor domains have significant implications in the learning process, the focus of a significant portion of educational assessment at the graduate level is on the cognitive domain.

Cognitive Domain

Almost from day one in most graduate programs, learners begin hearing about Bloom's Taxonomy. Questions are asked in the courseroom with the taxonomy in mind and more important, student discussions and assignments are assessed in large measure based on the taxonomy. Clearly, the taxonomy is a critical grading component of the comprehensive exam to assess learners' proficiency level in the higher order regions. Yet, most programs are not truly referring to the three domains within the taxonomy. They are speaking to a six stage, hierarchal framework of critical thinking and problem solving within the cognitive domain, also known as Bloom's Taxonomy of the Cognitive Domain.

Evaluation

Synthesis

Analysis

Application

Comprehension

Knowledge

The taxonomy provides specific definitions for each of the six major classifications in this domain. The categories are knowledge, comprehension, application, analysis, synthesis, and evaluation. The categories are ordered from simple to more complex higher level thinking skills. The hierarchy begins with knowledge and simple recall and progresses to an ability to create and evaluate on a scholarly level. The taxonomy is predicated on the belief that proficiency in each category is required before ascending to the next level.

The first category is knowledge. Knowledge refers to the ability to recall information that was previously learned. The second category, comprehension, refers to the capacity to understand and grasp the knowledge. The next progression, application, refers to the application of the knowledge to a problem solving. Analysis, the fourth region, refers to the scholarly dissection of the knowledge to include supporting evidence, nuances, and implications. The next category, synthesis, refers to the ability to actually create something new out of the analysis of previously learned knowledge. Lastly, evaluation refers to the highest level, which is the capacity to judge the merit and worth of the knowledge. These six categories of cognitive skills are a key component of the entire comprehensive exam phase.

Nexus to Comprehensive Exam

Comprehensive exams generally have three components. The first is the preamble, which lays the foundation for the rest of the question. The preamble will be in the form of a statement and should be afforded time and space in the comps response. The preamble is followed by lower level question and lastly, a higher order question.

In a doctoral comps question, the lower level sub-question may be in the application or analysis regions. I have seen some actually in the knowledge and comprehension categories. The higher order sub-question more than likely will be in the synthesis or evaluation region. Again, verbs such as synthesize or evaluate are obvious dead give-aways, but other verbs such as formulate, design, or assess also provide clues as to what level response the question requires. The following table may provide a better picture of the distinctions between the six cognitive classifications.

Cognitive Level	Descriptor	Associated Verbs
Knowledge	Memorization and recall	name list describe recall identify
Comprehension	Understanding	interpret discuss paraphrase differentiate compare
Application	Application of knowledge to practical situation	illustrate apply practice solve classify
Analysis	Examination of components	analyze appraise examine discriminate investigate
Synthesis	Rearrangement of knowledge into something unique	create predict design propose determine

Let me be very clear about the relevance between the comps exam and higher order critical thinking skills. While the grading rubric for a typical exam will consist of several elements such as logic, organization, flow, structure, and APA, the number one element is critical thinking. Your graders will be looking for you to demonstrate that you possess the necessary critical thinking skills to effectively and ethically conduct doctoral research and prepare a dissertation.

Continuing Relevance of the Taxonomy

Research conducted since Bloom and his associates developed the original taxonomy consistently has supported the taxonomy as a predictive hierarchy with the exception of the two higher order regions. It is a matter of debate whether synthesis and evaluation should be reversed as it can be argued that evaluation is a lesser complex thinking skill than synthesis, which refers to the capacity to actually create something new. In 2001, Anderson and Krathwohl offered a revised Bloom's taxonomy that recognized this reversal. Many scholars would suggest, at minimum, these two problem solving skills are on the same cognitive level albeit they have different approaches (Huitt, 2004).

Regardless of your position in this debate, one thing is clear. Both of these complex intellectual abilities are needed at the doctoral level. At minimum, one builds upon the other. At best they serve as perfect complements.

Chapter

16

Strategies for Success

Preparation

First things first...clear your schedule of any major events or travel during the comps time frame. A friend of mine had his daughter's wedding during his comps phase. I think he slept about 20 hours a week while taking the comps not to mention his mind was completely preoccupied. I do not suggest telling your daughter not to get married because you have a test to take, but you can postpone the comps until the following quarter. You have to take this phase of the doctoral program very seriously. Failing the comps is not a good experience. At many universities, learners are disenrolled from the university after failing the initial exam and one additional re-write opportunity.

Take the time to read everything about the comprehensive exam offered by your university or specific program. Most universities have a wealth of information for learners to read and study. One of your most important preparatory readings should be the scoring matrix. Make sure you understand the criteria upon which the committee will be evaluating your paper. Similarly, don't be afraid to ask learners or graduates who have passed the comps to share their strategies or advice. You will not be able to use them once you receive the questions, but they may be a wealth of information in preparing for the exam.

Make sure you are prepared with regard to content. If your program requires a one day test, you need to spend months preparing. Read everything on your reading list. Remember, scholarly reading does not necessarily involved word for word comprehension. *Skim and go* may be your best route until you get to the very specific theories and models. Many learners also find it beneficial to form study groups prior to the exam. This enables individual members to tackle a specific issue in more depth and share the information with the group.

If your exam follows the take home, open book philosophy, you still will need to study hard. The rigor with regard to grading obviously will be much harder with much more scrutiny. Frankly, a comprehensive exam in this model should not have to be perfect, but it should not be far from it. Keep this in mind as it is nearly impossible to prepare three or four doctoral level papers in the limited time you will be afforded, particularly when most learners are adults with all the normal work and family responsibilities. I actually took a week of vacation while writing my comps to finish them on time. Before the comps time clock starts clicking, review all of your past course papers and references. Update your references concerning topics that you know will be part of the exam such as research methods. And read everything your school offers regarding the comps phase. Many universities have very detailed manuals to assist learners with every aspect and expectation of the comprehensive exam. The bottom line is to do everything you can before the clock starts.

Follow Directions

You will have a specified time limit to prepare your responses. The specific timelines will vary from school to school and program to program. The one constant is that your exam will not be accepted after the specified deadline.

The second very important direction to follow is the page limit. I remember the first comprehensive exam I graded. At that time, the manuscript page count could not exceed 60 pages. The entire package was 80 pages with 70 pages of manuscript. I called the committee chair and asked how to handle this overrun of pages. "Is this page number thing something we really enforce?" Her response was very clear. "Stop reading after 60 pages of manuscript!" So, on the 60th page, which was the first page of the final response, I stopped reading. Obviously, the student did not fully answer the question in the first page, so the exam failed. My friends, fight with all of your might the urge to ramble. Redundancy and unnecessary information will doom a comps exam.

Conversely, savvy students use every bit of their allotted time and space. More often than receiving papers that are too long, I receive exams that are way too short. It already is nearly impossible to fully answer a doctoral comps question in 15-17 pages. I wonder if students really expect to pass the exam when they submit a six page response. Comps graders do appreciate a learner's ability to synthesize the literature into a small package, but six pages is not synthesis; it is a lack of commitment, energy, and appreciation of the process.

Writing the Responses

While strong preparation and adherence to the directions is a great start, there are some best practices with regard to writing your responses. The first is to make sure you respond appropriately to the question being asked.

As mentioned in Chapter 14, each comps question will have three components: preamble, lower level question, and higher level question. Be sure you understand all three components and be sure to address all three areas including the preamble.

I read and grade comprehensive exams very frequently. The surest way to fail is not to answer the comps question. As ridiculous as this sounds, I frequently read great papers – great content, great writing. Yet, the responses do not answer the comps question. I have had nicely written papers that only afforded a paragraph to the third component of the comps question, which is the higher order and arguably, the most important sub-question. Giving a synthesis or evaluation sub-question one paragraph of your time is a quick route to a failing grade. It may be human nature to write about what you know or wish the question had asked, but you have to fight that urge. Address the question and all of its components as it is posed.

Time Management

It is very easy to let the first week or even two go by having done very little with regard to actual writing. Do not let this happen! Take a couple of days to fully digest the questions, but then start writing. You have to learn to think and write at the same time in this phase.

Similarly, do not spend an inordinate amount of time on one question leaving little time to write the others. The specific method to handle this aspect will differ among different learners. A colleague of mine answered her hardest comps question first. Her position was that it would be more beneficial to get the hard stuff over so she could relax a bit while answering the remaining questions. I took the opposite approach. I tackled the easier questions first so I would have plenty of time for the tough one. Let me be clear; there were no easy comps questions. Yet, there were three in which I possessed a fairly solid foundation, and one I had absolutely no knowledge base. I wrote the first three fairly expeditiously, which allowed me the extra time I desperately needed for the more difficult question.

Additionally, prepare your reference page as you go. I have a friend who writes her entire paper, then painstakingly goes back through every citation to create her reference page. This really seems inefficient to me. It is quicker and more accurate to prepare your reference pages as you go. Every time you cite a source, go to the end of the document and type the appropriate reference.

My last words of wisdom about timeliness are to make sure you leave enough time for pristine proofreading. If your exam is due in four weeks, set your deadline at three weeks. That will give you a little cushion to read and re-read your papers for content issues and writing errors. There is nothing more frustrating for committee readers than to have to read a doctoral level comps exam replete with typos. Bad writing and inattention to the gravity of this exam are immediate re-writes with me. And remember, this is an exam. You cannot have others proofread it for you.

Writing 101

Even though the writing in a comprehensive exam is scholarly and very formal, the basic rules of writing an essay remain constant. Provide the reader a logical introduction, body of the paper, and conclusion. For each response, establish a central theme and align it with a logical and supported argument. Pay particular attention to the writing style manual adopted by your program or school. A comps exam does not have to be perfect to pass, but the writing and adherence to your style manual have to be pristine. Make sure to proofread and edit your responses several times before submitting them. Many comprehensive exams have typos and misspelled words, which are completely unacceptable at this level.

Plagiarism

I will be very brief here because Chapter 10 was devoted to plagiarism in its entirety. Yet, it is worthwhile to mention academic dishonesty in the context of the comprehensive exam. At most online universities and certainly at many brick and mortar schools, your comps exam will be submitted to an Internet based plagiarism detection service. Additionally, comps readers (graders) have a significant level of expertise in their discipline with a sound understanding and appreciation of the existing literature in that field. Comps readers frequently see issues of plagiarism just as faculty members do in the courseroom. Please re-familiarize yourself with the nuances and intricacies of plagiarism before writing and submitting your comps exam. I know of no faster route to failure than using others' ideas without proper attribution.

Comprehensive exam readers and the university have to have a significant level of trust in the learner before they can in good conscience elevate the learner to the dissertation phase. The dissertation has tremendous ethical considerations throughout the entire project and is completed with little direct oversight. The dissertation phase entails too many opportunities to harm the university's reputation or, much more importantly, harm the human participants in the study. Unethical conduct in the dissertation phase also can lead to inaccurate and misleading results being provided to the scientific community. Quite simply, if the comps readers do not have a strong level of trust in the learner's sense of morality or capacity to adhere to ethical behavior, they must not pass the learner to the dissertation phase.

Sources

As with the previous section, I will avoid the urge to go into detail here because Chapter 9 discusses appropriate scholarly sources in more depth. Yet, I do think it is worthwhile to emphasize the topic again with regard to the comprehensive exam. Committee readers will look at your citations and references. This is the very first thing I do when grading a comprehensive exam. They will look for APA, but more importantly, they will assess the types of sources you used to support your positions. As mentioned in Chapter 9, readers are not looking for specific numbers, but your paper should be replete with timely and relevant scholarly sources. Your papers also should avoid secondary sources at almost all costs. Scholars go straight to the original source. Lastly, make sure to actually use citations! This may sound crazy, but I still see plenty of exams that go on and on making assertions yet without providing any attribution. Here's a comment I wrote on a fairly recent exam. "Your first paragraph demonstrated probably the most significant flaw a doctoral learner can have. You offered numerous assertions (facts). Yet, you provided no citations. In fact, your entire introduction and entire conclusion, as well as countless paragraphs throughout the paper, do not have citations. You should have learned very early, even at the Masters level, that scholarly writing is about exploring the literature (citations) and then using critical thinking skills to analyze, synthesize, and evaluate. When you offer facts with no citations, it is your opinion or experience, or it is plagiarism. None of these three is acceptable at the graduate level much less the doctoral level." Lack of quality citations will doom a comps exam.

Rewrites

Obviously the percentages will differ among universities and programs, but certainly, not all learners pass the comprehensive exam with their first attempt. Many programs allow learners a second opportunity to pass, a rewrite. Some programs require learners to take the entire exam over even if they only fail one question. Others will allow the learner to rewrite only the response(s) that did not receive a passing score on the first attempt. Either way, not passing the comps on the first try can be emotionally devastating because with many programs, a twice no-pass means the learner will not be allowed to progress to the dissertation phase. Some schools will offer the learner a master's degree at this point in recognition of the learner's successful completion of their course work and comprehensive exam. Bottom line is that learners who do not pass the comps cannot continue their doctoral studies.

Some learners know from the beginning that their work will not pass. Time ran out or a crisis arose mid way through the process, and they count on passing the rewrite. However, most learners are completely taken by surprise when they receive a non-passing score. If you are required to rewrite your exam, take a deep break and compose yourself. This is not the end. The majority of learners do indeed pass the comps by the second attempt. A rewrite will require your best work, complete focus, and attention to every detail of the reviewers' remarks. Read the comments from reviewers very carefully. Address every single issue. Do not spend time thinking about how the reviewers might be wrong. Don't dwell in disappointment or anger. Focus, review, research, and rewrite. A very high percentage of rewrites are successful. Do all you can to make sure you are one of the successes!

As a Final Recap...

Four *Musts* with Comprehensive Exams

1. Be honest. This should go without saying, but faculty graders still see blatant plagiarism in comps exams, which obviously has serious consequences.

2. Write scholarly and use scholarly sources. Adhere to APA or your program's desired writing manual and proofread your paper over and over.

3. Display higher order critical thinking and problem solving skills with regard to Bloom's Taxonomy - synthesis and evaluation at the doctoral level.

4. Fully answer the comps question addressing all three components of the question!

Part
VI

Bringing It Home

Completing the
Dissertation

Continuous effort –
not strength or intelligence –
is the key to unlocking our potential.

Winston Churchill

The dissertation is the capstone of the doctoral degree. It is the requirement through which the knowledge and insights gained through the courses and comprehensive exam are brought to bear to conduct original research. For me, this was the most exciting part of the doctoral journey. The dissertation provided the opportunity to actually contribute something new and of value to my field. I chose a topic that has interested me for years and continues to spark my curiosity. Yet, so many learners struggle with this stage. The independent nature of this phase and relative lack of structure combine to provide an environment that can be very challenging for some students.

Obviously, most people do not have a Ph.D. and still lead happy, rewarding lives and make important contributions to their community. Many do quite well financially for themselves without a formal education. However, this is not the path you chose. You embarked on something special and unique. You worked long and hard to get here. You have come too far now to turn back. Although my excitement never wavered during the dissertation phase, there were many times when either the amount of work or the many obstacles and traps along the way made life very tough and frustrating. Yet, I never gave in and neither will you!

What 'Not' to Expect from Part VI

Numerous books are available to help you tackle the dissertation. Books such as Writing the Winning Dissertation by Allan Glatthorn, Social Research by Morley Glicken, and Research Design by John Creswell are excellent sources that provide specific guidance. Thus, the purpose of Part VI is not to provide a detailed guide to navigating the dissertation process. What Part VI offers is an overview of the dissertation and the dissertation process and valuable insights and strategies based on years of experience from seasoned dissertation committee and research faculty. Part VI does dive into one subject with some detail: Ethical Research in the Social Sciences. As this is a crucial subject for doctoral learners to understand, and the fact that it gets limited attention in many dissertation books, compelled me to include the subject here.

So, what's all the fuss about this thing called a dissertation? Isn't it just a book that doctoral students write before graduation?

Chapter 17

What is a Dissertation?

Intuition may be fine for buying stocks or falling in love...but in the real world of the social scientist, intuition may neither help us understand issues that confront us nor serve to provide needy people with the most effective service possible.

Dr. Morley D. Glicken

The journey to earning a doctorate is unique in that it culminates with a scholarly challenge to deeply explore an important topic or problem in the learner's chosen discipline. The truly differentiating aspect of this exploration is that students are required to conduct original or primary research. In other words, doctoral candidates contribute something that has never been done before! Dr. Peter Fiske observed, "In the Ph.D., you are tasked with marching to the cliff's edge of what is known in a particular field, gazing down into the vast abyss of the unknown, and taking the next step. It's amazing, if you think about it."

Purpose of the Dissertation

The dissertation is the final right of passage for those wishing to enter into the select world of doctoral scholars. In this sense, the main purpose of a dissertation is to graduate. The dissertation demonstrates to the university and other Ph.D.s (the committee) that learners have attained the knowledge and capacity to apply that knowledge at a scholarly level. It demonstrates that these students know how to conduct primary research, have produced something new and of value to the discipline, and have communicated that research at a doctoral level both orally and in writing. While the dissertation represents an impression of finality in this respect, it also represents a beginning as new Ph.D.s are now equipped to make valuable, innovative contributions to society for many years to come.

The dissertation also serves another purpose. The skills learners develop and enhance during the dissertation phase will stay with them a lifetime. These experiences help them to better appreciate research, create new research, publish in various formats, and successfully lecture on their dissertation topic. The entire dissertation process, from a thorough review of the literature to the actual new research and implications, provides a specific base of knowledge that few others will possess.

The Heart of a Dissertation

Dissertations have three overarching requirements. They must be unique, important, and valuable. *Unique* means that the study is simply not an exact duplication or interpretation of a previous study. Maybe you will use different instruments than other studies. Maybe you will tap into a different population than previous research. Dissertations do not have to be earth shattering innovations, but they must represent some level of "moving the ball forward" in your chosen discipline.

Important means the project has relevance and significance to the discipline. Many occasions during the developmental stages, the dissertation chair or committee members will ask, "So what?" They are not being flippant or rude. They are trying to get to the heart of whether or not the topic is important.

> *...you should view the dissertation as something more than an unpleasant requirement – what some students disparagingly call "the fee for the union card." You should see it also as a way of learning.*
>
> Dr. Allan A. Glatthorn

Valuable infers that the study provides data and insights that are of worth to the discipline. Similar to the *so what* question, committees also will ask, "Who cares?" Again, they are just trying to get at the value of the project.

Organization

Dissertations come in differing shapes, sizes, formats, and styles. I have seen dissertations ranging from four chapters to six. I have seen dissertations that were 100 pages and others near 400. The determination to go with a quantitative or qualitative approach also will have bearing on the format, look, and even page count of the dissertation.

I remember asking my dissertation chair how many pages he was expecting from my quantitative dissertation. He said something to the effect, "I don't care how many pages it turns out to be. Write until it's done – no more, no less. But, I have to tell you Jeff. There's something wrong with your ability to write and synthesize at the doctoral level if you can't get this done in 150 pages." He was smiling when he said this, but he was serious too. Dissertations have a certain level of redundancy. This is needed so that each chapter can stand on its own while still being an integral part of the whole. However, dissertations should not be extra wordy. Learners have to write in a coherent, scholarly manner and fight the temptation to pour irrelevant information in the document.

Many universities and committees let doctoral candidates choose what specific format works best for them. Many colleges will have templates to use as a guideline, while still affording a great deal of autonomy to the student. Having said this, almost all dissertations will contain the following components in some fashion:

The Chapters

Again, the number of chapters, title of the chapters, and specific composition of the chapters will differ from school to school and person to person. Quantitative studies tend to follow a similar, more traditional structure, while qualitative studies may need much more flexibility depending on the type of research (case study, action research, etc.) Having said this, in my experience the most common format is the five chapter approach: Statement of the problem, review of the literature, methodology, data analysis and results, and summary and discussion.

Statement of the Problem

The first chapter introduces the study and establishes the overarching problem that the dissertation will address. It may be appropriate in some dissertations to provide a background of the problem. The introduction also should describe the purpose and significance of the research. Most introductions will discuss the research paradigm and provide several research questions that guided the entire project. Key terms and definitions should be addressed as well as assumptions and limitations of the research. Introductions may conclude with a brief summary or an overview of the organization of the dissertation.

Literature Review

The literature review provides an in depth summary of the existing research and current base of knowledge concerning the direction of the current dissertation. Yet, the literature review provides more than just an unbiased, comprehensive summary. It offers a critical

---

Common Dissertation Components

- Title page

- Copyright page

- Signature page

- Abstract

- Dedication

- Acknowledgments

- Contents

- List of Tables and Figures

- The Chapters

- References

- Appendices

---

analysis and evaluation of the existing literature in light of theoretical, empirical, and practical concerns. As David Boote and Penny Beile (2005) commented, "A thorough, sophisticated literature review is the foundation and inspiration for substantial, useful research."

The literature review has a dual role. The first is to demonstrate to the committee that the learner possesses a thorough understanding and appreciation of the existing literature concerning the topic and discipline. The second role of the literature review is to position the dissertation with respect to prior studies. It serves to show the relevance of previous research with regard to the current dissertation. In other words, it gives the reader a sense of context as to how you (and your discipline) got to where you are.

It is these reasons why many dissertation faculties view the review of the literature as the most important component of the dissertation. I even would suggest that the literature review (at least some sort of draft) be written before any other chapters. The research that goes into this process will bode well for you as you work through the other chapters and begin to decide on which research perspective, method, even instruments and sample, will best suit your topic.

Methodology

The methodology chapter, generally Chapter 3, may begin with a brief overview of the methodology. The research perspective and design also should be addressed. Although mentioned in the introductory chapter, this is the place where the dissertation substantively articulates whether the study is quantitative, qualitative, or a blended methodology. This is very important to the reader as these different research perspectives develop from different epistemologies. Quantitative methods imply that an objective reality exists that can be measured with numbers. Examples would include experimental, correlational, or evaluative research. Conversely, qualitative methods imply that reality rests in people's perceptions. The focus of a qualitative study would then be on deeply understanding and appreciating the nuances and meaning of the topic as opposed to a heavy reliance on statistical analysis. A few examples would include action, ethnographic, or case study research.

This chapter also may include a section on the research context if needed for the reader to fully grasp the setting and population. Two of the most important components of this chapter are the sampling design and instrumentation. Remember, the readers of your dissertation probably are scholars in the discipline who know the literature and understand sound research. They will want to be able to readily access why you chose your particular sample, and why you chose to use particular assessments or measurement procedures. Further, they will want to be able to quickly evaluate the validity and reliability of the instruments, which also should be addressed in this chapter. Similarly, this chapter should discuss the data collection and analysis scheme.

Presentation and Data Analysis/Results

The results chapter generally begins with a brief restatement of the purpose as well as the research questions. In fact, a good way to organize this chapter is to provide the results of the study with regard to each individual question. The heart of this chapter is to articulate the statistical tests used to make sense of the data and why those measures were chosen. For example, chi square may be the best test for descriptive analysis whereas the Pearson Product Moment Correlation may be the most appropriate for continuous variables. This chapter, particularly with a quantitative study, will be replete with tables and charts. The idea with the results chapter is to present the main results of the research in a scholarly fashion and provide evidence to justify the conclusions.

Discussion

Many discussion chapters begin with a re-statement of the problem and a review of the methodology. The heart of this chapter, however, is that the results described in the data analysis chapter are summarized with scholarly interpretations in the context of the study's research questions. This chapter allows, actually requires, that the learner qualify the results, make inferences from them, and discuss the potential theoretical and practical implications. This chapter generally concludes with a discussion of the limitations of the research as well as recommendations for future research.

The Dissertation Committee

The dissertation committee usually comprises between three and five members of whom one will be the chair (also referred to as the doctoral advisor or doctoral mentor). The composition of the committee will vary from program to program, but generally, most schools like a mixture of expertise on the committee. For example, on my committee I had a chair and two faculty members. One of the members had an expertise in methodology and the institutional review board (IRB) process and another member had expertise in my dissertation topic (personality and leadership). Additionally, I sought out the guidance of a fourth faculty member who had an expertise in statistics although he was not officially on the committee.

One of the best aspects of online learning is that the hierarchal games of academe generally are not present. A dissertation committee in many traditional programs may consist of similarly diverse members with diverse ranks as well. One may be a full professor, one may be an instructor, or one may be an assistant professor. I have had numerous Ph.D.s tell me that member status can be an obstacle to the learner's success because of organizational politics, particularly if a committee member outranks the chair. In the online environment, this type of squabbling and attention to rank has no standing. In fact, your dissertation chair may be an adjunct faculty member with the two other committee members being core faculty. Because the chair would not be the chair without substantial experience and credentials, the two full-time faculty members would treat her exactly as if the roles were reversed. I still have an affinity for face-to-face education, but this is just one more benefit that online learning has over brick and mortar programs that remain glued to tradition and the failed paradigm of "we've always done it this way."

The Oral Defense

Writing the dissertation almost gets you home. But there is one more aspect of fully completing the dissertation phase. You must orally defend it to your committee. There are all sorts of strategies to making it through the defense such as preparing a power point presentation or even bringing donuts. Possibly the best strategy is to actually sit in on a couple of oral defenses if your school allows this. As opposed to offering specific guidance in this section regarding the oral defense, I just want to point out a couple of aspects of the defense you may find helpful.

The first reflects a distinction between many traditional and online programs. With many brick and mortar programs, the dissertation is submitted to the full committee shortly (usually just a few weeks) before the defense. While the chair has had months to critique the document, the full committee receives it just in time to read and fully digest it before the oral defense. Obviously, during the oral defense, the committee members will have many questions and generally will make numerous suggestions to make the document acceptable. The learner then goes back to work on the dissertation to shore up the problem areas identified by the committee. While this may occur on rare occasions in the online environment, the typical path of the oral defense is much different. Obviously the chair is much more involved with the dissertation than the full committee in either context, yet in the online setting, the whole committee works with the learner throughout the entire dissertation. More to the point, the full committee must approve the dissertation *before* the oral defense is scheduled. The crucial benefit of this strategy is that the oral defense in this scenario is not about the dissertation as much as it is about the learner's ability to discuss the dissertation and all its components, particularly the chapter five implications.

While my comprehensive exam oral defense was a brutal challenge, I always will remember my dissertation oral defense as a positive, professional, and collegiate experience. Although I was asked some very thought provoking questions, it was not adversarial in the least. As I was the one who had spent months and months conducting this research and reviewing the literature, I actually was viewed as the subject matter expert at the table. It was almost like four colleagues sitting around a table at Starbucks discussing the intricacies of a topic and research study of which we all shared a common passion. That's the way an oral defense should be!

Final Thoughts

What do you call a learner who barely squeaked his dissertation past his committee?   Doctor. ☺

You all have heard about the army of ABDs (all but dissertation) sprinkled throughout our society. These students made it through the course work and the comprehensive exam but just never quite made it through the dissertation phase. The reasons for this are plentiful and often may be beyond the control of the student. However, possibly the largest barriers to completing the dissertation are learners' inherent need for perfection and their desire to contribute something of incredible value to the world. As we move through the next two chapters, consider the wisdom I was offered during the initial stages of my dissertation.

A professor from a local, brick and mortar university offered me some very sage advice. "There are two types of dissertations – A really great one and a finished one. Go with the finished one, Jeff!" I have heard similar advice given to students many times over the years. I am not for one minute advocating that you should go down the path of least resistance. I am not advocating short cuts or less than quality work. Indeed, your chair, committee, and school review process will make sure your work is of a high quality. All I am suggesting is to prepare a worthy dissertation of significance and value to your discipline but to save the multi-year, save the world research for after graduation.

Chapter

18

Research
Ethics
in the
Social
Sciences

Scientific research offers tremendous benefits to both practitioners and consumers. Indeed, much of what is known about the social sciences is gained through intensive research using focus groups, surveys, interviews, ethnographies, historical data, participant observation and a range of other research methods. Research can help establish effective approaches and treatments. Research also can help determine the efficacy of existing interventions. Research can assist all decision makers in gaining the necessary knowledge to make intelligent choices.

Understanding the implications associated with research is an absolute necessity for learners. Graduate programs require learners to take methodology courses that address, to some extent, ethical issues in research. Many programs require additional classes such as the Collaborative Institutional Training Initiative (CITI) course. Doctoral candidates must appreciate their enormous ethical responsibilities. They have to understand the consequences of breaching the trust of the scientific community and society when research does not meet the highest standards for ethical protection of human participants.

While social research has offered significant benefits for society, it also has cast disturbing doubts regarding the ethical treatment of human participants. Researchers continually must weigh the potential benefits of research endeavors against the potential harm it may cause to individuals and society.

The Impetus of Safeguarding Polices

Numerous research efforts over the past half century resulted in the unethical exploitation of human participants. Milgram's (1963) research on obedience and authority, the Willowbrook Hepatitis study wherein mentally retarded children were injected with hepatitis (Beecher, 1996), and Humphreys's (1975) ethnographic research focusing on homosexual encounters in public restrooms are commonly recognized as stunning examples of the unethical treatment of research participants by researchers.

Two studies in particular served as watershed events in bringing ethical issues to the international forefront of research practices. The most notable study came to attention after World War II with the discovery of a wide variety of abusive biomedical experiments conducted at Nuremberg. Among other atrocities, children, for example, were injected with malaria and typhus.

Another horrendous endeavor in the name of research was the Public Health Service Syphilis Study (also known as the Tuskegee Syphilis experiment) in which over 100 African-American men died of syphilis and other associated complications. This 40 year study, which included the intentional withholding of lifesaving penicillin from participants, embodied the ethical abuses in human research of the past and continues to serve as a beacon of caution for potential ethical misconduct in the future (Thomas & Quinn, 1991).

The attention brought as a result of Nuremburg, Tuskegee, and other studies appropriately forced researchers to institute standards and practices to assist in the ethical protection of human subjects involved in research. The Code of Nuremberg, which delineated specific elements required for research using human subjects, was established in 1947 to bring clarity to vague and conflicting guidelines that existed prior to Nazi Germany. The Helsinki Declaration of 1964 was another landmark move towards improving the ethical safeguards established to protect human participants in research. It was this decree by the World Medical Association that precipitated the eventual establishment of institutional review boards. In 1974, Congress enacted the National Research Act that called for the establishment of the National Commission for the Protection of Human Subjects of Biomedical and Behavioral Research. The National Commission produced the *Belmont Report* in 1979 in an effort to offer fundamental ethical guidance towards resolving ethical dilemmas with research involving human participants.

The United States government did something that was wrong - deeply, profoundly, morally wrong. It was an outrage to our commitment to integrity and equality for all our citizens...
The people who ran the study at Tuskegee diminished the stature of man by abandoning the most basic ethical precepts.

President Clinton's apology for the
Tuskegee Syphilis Experiments
May 16, 1997

Ethical Values in Social Research

As early as the 1920s, an array of rules and regulations existed around the world concerning the protection of human subjects in research. However, these rules were often too inflexible or too vague to be of any real value. The significance of the Belmont Report was that it established a consistency with regard to values. The main values provided in the report are (a) respect for persons, (b) beneficence and non-malfeasance, and (c) justice.

Respect for Persons

According to the Belmont Report, capable individuals should be afforded deference to their considered judgments. Respect for individuals demands that potential participants are provided the knowledge needed to make informed decisions regarding participation in the research. Sensitivity to issues of confidentiality and privacy are also important elements of respect.

The principle of respect protects persons not capable of self-determination such as the emotionally or mentally incapacitated. Researchers also must consider other vulnerable populations such as pregnant women and prisoners. Respect for individuals appropriately focuses the attention on an "informed, competent, and voluntary participant" (Kalmbach & Lyons, 2003, p. 677).

Beneficence and Nonmalfeasance

The concept of beneficence, to do good, and nonmalfeasance, to do no harm, has been a long-standing ethical mandate within the Hippocratic tradition of medicine. Antle and Regehr (2003) caution that consideration should include anticipated physical risks as well as private concerns such as embarrassment, anguish, or reputation. Social researchers must be particularly sensitive to such social stigmas.

Justice

Justice is a value based on equality. Justice demands that individuals are treated in an impartial, fair, and consistent manner. The value of justice has many implications in the field of social research. For example, providing more information about risks of the study to one potential participant than to another would be contrary to the principle of justice. The ethical selection of participants also is a consideration under the value of justice. As noted in the Belmont Report, during the early twentieth century, indigent hospital patients often served as research participants while wealthier patients were the recipients of the enhanced medical treatments. As researchers should not take advantage of vulnerable individuals, they also should not reject participants without just cause who may gain from participation in the research. It is these principles that establish the context for the policies and practices employed today in research ethics.

Protecting Human Subjects in Research

Ethical failures may arise in research due to immoral behaviors such as misrepresenting data or incorrectly reporting results. However, more often than not, my sense is that lapses occur because researchers fail to follow established guidelines. Informed consent and the advent of institutional review boards are two of the most encompassing policies that have been established in an attempt to reduce ethical failures in research.

Informed Consent

Respect for individuals is at the core of ethical research. The policy of informed consent is at the center of this value. The goal of informed consent is to provide research participants a clear method of communication regarding the study.

> *Who ought to receive the benefits of research and bear its burdens? This is a question of justice, in the sense of "fairness in distribution" or "what is deserved."*
>
> *The Belmont Report*

The three central components of informed consent are information, understanding of that information, and voluntary consent to participate in the study.

Information

The first element of informed consent is that potential participants are provided with sufficient information necessary to make an informed decision. The following items comprise informed consent (Creswell, 2003; American Psychological Association [APA], 2001):

- The identification of the researcher
- The nature and role of the research
- The research procedures
- Expected duration of the study
- Potential hazards and benefits
- A confidentiality statement

Most informed consent forms will include language acknowledging the participants entitlement to ask questions and leave the study at any time. Additionally, some policies require the researcher to provide the results of the study to participants at its conclusion.

Possibly the most important aspect of informed consent is that it initiates a dialogue between the researcher and participant. It is during this exchange that the person begins to make sense of the information, and the researcher begins to assess the capacity of the subject to understand the information and make reasonable, self-determinate decisions accordingly,

Understanding

The second element of informed consent is the capacity of the participant to comprehend the information provided by the researcher, including potential risks, benefits, and predictable consequences of accepting or declining involvement in the study. This element is rooted in the value of respect for an individual's dignity. The

> *In any research on human beings, each potential subject must be adequately informed of the aims, methods, sources of funding, any possible conflicts of interest, institutional affiliations of the researcher, the anticipated benefits and potential risks of the study and the discomfort it may entail.*
>
> *Helsinki Declaration*

first intended protection of this element is that of the self-determination of capable decision makers. This necessitates an honest presentation of the information by the researcher in a language and at a comprehension level commensurate with the abilities of the participant. It also requires that potential participants are provided with enough time to permit them to fully judge the merits of their involvement.

The second intention of this element is the protection of potential research participants who lack the capacity to make informed, responsible choices on their own behalf. Consideration is given to such characteristics as the participant's age, mental capacity, emotional stability, and maturity. Extreme vigilance must be taken to ensure that susceptible groups, such as children and the mentally ill, are not exploited.

Voluntariness

The third component of informed consent is the voluntary nature of participant involvement. Voluntariness demands freedom of choice. Participants should be able to make their determinations without the intrusion of any aspect of power, hoax, duress, overreaching, or other hidden types of coercion or undue influence by the researcher (Backlar, 1998). Participants must be aware that their involvement is not only initially voluntary, but that they may withdraw at any time during the study.

Coercion usually appears when researchers make threats to gain participation in a study. Coercion generally presents in situations where potential participants of a study do not operate in an independent fashion such as those in prisons or mental health institutions. Undue influence, by comparison, appears when researchers make inappropriate offers to gain participation in the study. This is not to suggest that paying research subjects for their participation is unethical. The unethical nature of the issue arises when the payment is inappropriately too high.

Informed consent is largely administered through a variety of guidelines, federal regulations, and volunteer endeavors. However, steps have been taken to bring informed consent to a higher level of standardization. Possibly the most significant policy towards this end is the advent of the formalized research review process most recognized as the institutional review board.

Institutional Review Board (IRB)

In 1974, the United States became the first country to mandate that all institutions receiving federal monies must tender research proposals involving human participants to a local review board. Institutions not receiving federal funds may still be required to establish IRBs, also referred to as ethics or human subjects review boards, by other private regulatory bodies such as the American Psychological Association.

The purpose of an IRB is to provide a formal ethical review of a research study prior to its implementation. Every university has an IRB and school specific processes that align with the overall university IRB. It is worth noting that many other organizations have IRBs as well that you may have to address. For example, I had to submit an IRB application to both my university and the Department of Justice/ FBI because I was conducting research in FBI space. Moreover, I had additional ethical concerns to address because my sample comprised students (even though their average age was 41).

The CFR (1991, §46.111) provides five mandates that must be fulfilled prior to approval by an IRB. The prospective risk to participants must be minimal. The risks associated with the study also must be rational in regard to the anticipated good to participants and society. Ethical selection of research subjects is paramount. The tenets of informed consent must be followed and acknowledged in writing. Lastly, IRBs must develop further protections to shelter vulnerable and otherwise marginal populations from potential abuse.

Categories of Review

There are three common categories of review regarding research proposals and the IRB process: (a) exempt, (b) expedited, and (c) full board. Some types of research may be exempt from full review by IRBs. For example, research involving surveys or field interviews or personal observations are often exempt from full board review unless participants can be identified or the study focuses on highly personal domains of the partici-pant's conduct. An expedited review generally involves approval by a small sub-committee of the IRB. These types of stud-ies would pose a very minimal risk such as checking someone's height and weight, tak-ing voice recordings,

> *Coercion is characterized as such rational social interaction and exercise of power that the weaker party is threatened by the stronger party. The weaker party will suffer a loss whatever it does, and the stronger party will gain from such action.*
>
> *~Timo Airaksinen*

or the study of existing or archived data. Research proposals that do not meet the requirements of the exempt or expedited route need full IRB approval prior to implementation.

Other Ethics Review Formats

In addition to IRBs, there are two other types of ethics review committees. Proprietary review committees are established by private research entities to review their own research protocols. Non-institutional review boards are used to evaluate studies for researchers who are not associated with organizations that have an IRB. While these two forms of review are not mandated by law, they represent a strengthening of efforts towards the protection of human participants involved in research.

Final Thoughts

The many elements of informed consent and institutional review serve as powerful safeguards toward the protection of human subjects in research. However, there is indication that this scheme of ethical review may not sufficiently shield the rights of subjects. For example, Berg (1996) observed that no broadly established, empirically-based criterion exists to assist in deciding the worth of a participant's choice or sufficiency of comprehension. Often informed consent forms are too lengthy and complicated for ordinary research participants to truly understand. Possibly the worst failing of safeguarding policies is their lack of universal application. Discrepancies and gaps exist between federal and state laws governing research, and private research is often not guided by any governmental or professional association's code of ethics concerning informed consent or IRB procedures. Despite these limitations, informed consent and formal review committees represent salient growth toward establishing a community of researchers committed to accountable and ethical research involving human participants.

The exercise of ethics in social science research, as in other areas of human connectivity, often creates quandaries for which there are no obvious solutions. Possibly the greatest contribution of these protections is the continued attention they bring to the evolving journey of safeguarding the rights, well-being, and welfare of human participants in research.

> *...the university IRB delegates to each school the authority and responsibility to conduct the first review to determine whether the planned research involves the risk of psychological, social, or physical harm to human participants/ subjects. If the school representative to the IRB determines that there is the risk of harm, then the university IRB reviews the proposal and weighs the potential risk against the potential benefit of the research in order to approve or deny the proposal.*
>
> *Capella University Policy Statement*
> *Use of Human Participants/Subjects in Research*

Chapter

19

Strategies

for

Success

by

Dr. Curtis Brant

Associate Dean
School of Public Service Leadership
Capella University

Congratulations on making it to the dissertation! You have demonstrated to yourself and your university that you have the intelligence and persistence to begin the final chapter of your graduate studies, the dissertation. You will need to rely on your existing strengths and even develop some new skills along the way. Let's look at the skills, perceptions, and habits will you need to succeed.

Defining Success

I have, of course, completed my own dissertation, seen my own friends complete their dissertation, and supervised many dissertations. When I think about approaching a dissertation from my faculty role now, I liken it to taking on a new consulting project. The first thing one does when consulting is to help the individual or organization to define success. In defining success, we help to set expectations, needs, goals, and the processes by which we will reach those goals.

So, how can you begin to define success for your own dissertation? Let's approach this as though we were consultants looking at your situation. Without censoring your ideas, write a list of goals surrounding your dissertation. When you look over your list, you probably have personal and professional goals associated with the dissertation. For instance, success for you may mean a publication of your research in a scholarly journal or presentation of your work at a major professional conference.

You will recall earlier in the book, Dr. Green referred to a successful dissertation as a "completed" one. So, if you do not have *completed dissertation* on your list, I hope that you include it now. As this chapter is about providing guidance and tools to successfully *complete* your dissertation, let's use a "completed dissertation" as our initial definition of success.

Success can be measured in small steps too. It's easy when we view your dissertation from the outside to define success as a completed dissertation. Yet, for you, the learner working on your dissertation, one of the best things you can do is to realize that your dissertation is more than just a single written piece of text. It really is a process. The process of completing a dissertation is actually just a series of small steps. A dissertation has chapters. Before you can complete any one chapter, you must complete the paragraphs of that chapter, and before you complete each paragraph, you must complete each sentence. Although a completed dissertation is a major accomplishment, it is really nothing more than a collection of chapters, paragraphs, and at its basic level, sentences. Yes, a dissertation can be measured in completed sentences!

One of the biggest reasons why learners do not complete or struggle to complete a dissertation is that they become caught up in the complexity and grand scale of the overall task. They become paralyzed by fear because they cannot envision writing such a document. On the other hand, those learners who have completed their dissertation, and do it the fastest, work on small bits (sentences and paragraphs) each day. By breaking down a dissertation into its smaller components, it will be easier for you to reward yourself for accomplishments along the way to achieving your ultimate goals.

Preparing for Success

Now that you have had a chance to visualize what success looks like and how you can measure it, we need to plan for success. There are three significant components of this plan. First, you want to mentally prepare for the road ahead. Second, you want to establish a supportive and positive environment within which to work. Third, you want to give some thought to developing a writing schedule. Let's take each in turn.

Preparing Mentally

Completing your dissertation necessarily involves altering some of the ways you think and behave. You will change some of your views of the world. You will alter your work habits and schedule, and you will experience changes in your relationships. Recognizing and understanding these changes are the first steps in mentally preparing for your dissertation.

One model of change that I refer to often in my discussions with mentees is the Transtheoretical Model of Change. Prochaska and DiClemente (1983) proposed this extensively researched model of change most notably in its applications in the health care field.

However, the model has been used widely in other arenas, and I think it is applicable here as well. Essentially, they posit that change is a process that can be identified by a number of stages. The first of these stages is where individuals are unaware or unconcerned with approaching change. The individuals first must become aware of potential change and then begin to contemplate options for modifying their thoughts and behaviors (second stage). Once they have started thinking about the issues, they can assess their resources and develop a plan (third and fourth stages). After that plan has been implemented, the individuals must work to maintain (or revise) the plan to ensure the change remains persistent (fifth stage).

My guess is that most of you reading this chapter are in the first or second stage of change. You may be unaware of what is ahead and what is required (first stage), but hopefully in reading this book, you are becoming educated as to the road ahead and beginning to think about options for modifying your thoughts and behaviors (the second stage of change). You also are learning about planning and organization and how to start gathering the resources needed for your dissertation (the third stage of change). At some point sooner or later in your academic journey, you will take affirmative action by beginning to write your dissertation. It is at that point that you begin to put into play all of the resources you have compiled (the fourth stage of change). Finally, you must sustain your changes, motivation, and behaviors (the fifth stage of change) to be successful in reaching your goal of a completed dissertation.

Why is understanding this model of change important? In my experience, when learners struggle or fail to complete a dissertation, it is because they freeze from fear, or they want to jump right into action phase (the fourth stage of change in this theory) without giving due diligence to preparing for the change. By not adequately preparing, these learners do not use their available resources and tend to develop habits that are difficult to maintain or are just wrong. The dissertation is complex enough. You don't have to make it more complicated than it has to be because you were mentally unprepared for the journey.

Bottom line is this - You are growing and changing during the dissertation phase. Do not neglect this fact. Start preparing for this change by first recognizing it and then preparing yourself and your environment to support your resilience and persistence.

Preparing Your Environment

As a social psychologist, I can tell you there is a significant amount of scientific support for the notion that environment and situation impact our thoughts and behaviors (see seminal works by Festinger & Carlsmith, 1959 or Latane & Darly, 1968). Your friends, family, and co-workers will have an impact on your work. Similarly, your physical environment and writing space also will impact you. All too often, learners do not recognize the power of the situation in their own lives and do not plan adequately for how much of an impact external factors can have on their ability to complete their dissertation.

What can you do to prepare your environment? Let family know what you are doing. Be honest with your family that what you are doing is difficult, and that you will need some time to not only write but also to think. I recall my advisor's wife telling me once that when her husband was writing his dissertation, he would just walk around in the backyard for an hour or two after dinner trying to get his thoughts together. The family, of course, would wonder what was wrong with him. In actuality, there was nothing wrong with him; he just needed the time alone to think. Let your family know your needs so they can be supportive and encouraging of your new demands and subsequent habits.

Similarly, you may or may not want to let your friends and co-workers know what you are doing. Close friends and co-workers will know because of the change in you they undoubtedly will see. And close friends will support you and revel in your accomplishments. However, to be honest with you, not all people will look favorably on you while working on your dissertation. Some people will feel threatened. Some will not see the value in your efforts. For a variety of such reasons, not everyone will be supportive. Give some thought to who you tell about your work. This is not being secretive; it is thoughtfully planning your environment so that you surround yourself with positivity and support.

Finally, prepare your workspace. As you will read in the next section, I suggest you work on your dissertation everyday. Yes everyday! Where will you work on your dissertation? Are there spaces that are better for thinking? for writing? for editing? And don't forget, where ever you choose to work, be sure to surround yourself with the resources you will need for success.

Preparing Your Schedule

When I reflect on the time writing my dissertation, I recall one of my friends, Ken, who seemed to just sail through the entire process. At the time, it seemed like Ken was just better than me. I could not understand why things seemed to be so easy for him and so hard for me. All that changed one day when we were both in the computer lab writing, and we got to talking about our work. I was amazed to find that Ken had similar challenges as me; he just handled them differently. For one thing, Ken worked on his dissertation every day. Yes, that included holidays, birthdays, and anniversaries. Everyday meant everyday. He told me that he did not have to do a lot everyday, but he had to do something, whether it was writing a single sentence or writing a whole section of a chapter. Needless to say, I adopted Ken's strategy, and my outlook and persistence exponentially improved.

When I earned my first teaching position after receiving my doctorate, I was talking with one of the senior faculty members in my department. Amazingly, when she told me about how she completed her dissertation, she told me the same thing! She worked on the project everyday, and she kept her motivation high by frequently rewarding herself for those small accomplishments.

How can you reward yourself to maintain your schedule and perseverance? I recall one friend in graduate school often would think about what he needed to accomplish each day (for instance writing three paragraphs of the methodology). He would take a bite-size Three Musketeers candy bar (his favorite candy) and place it on top of his computer monitor while he was working. When he reached his goal for the day, he would eat the candy bar. This is a simple illustration, but it is rooted in a deep scientific history of the study of reinforcement and behavior. You only need to look in any introduction to psychology text to see an entire chapter devoted to methods of behavior modification. My point is that positive reinforcement works. Consider what motivates you and reward yourself when you accomplish your daily goals.

Preparing yourself mentally and preparing your environment for success are steps that ultimately will make the dissertation process more manageable. The next section covers some more concrete ways to help plan for your dissertation success.

Review the Guidelines for your Dissertation

The mental work that you will do as part of your dissertation is very challenging. After all, you are contributing something new to the scientific literature in your field. The analysis, synthesis, and evaluation of prior research and the construction of your own study present significant challenges. In my experience, the most successful learners are the ones who seek out and use their available resources. Resources that are available to you through your university, mentor, and fellow learners will not do the thinking for you, but they will help provide a solid structure, guide, and evaluation criteria that will be invaluable when writing your dissertation.

You might be surprised to learn that writing a dissertation is actually very formulaic. There are specific parts that must come before others. Certain information will appear over and over within the dissertation. Knowing where to put this information and why it goes in these places within the text allows you to focus your energy where it should be - on the content of the dissertation. Similarly, if you know how the dissertation will be evaluated by your mentor (chair) and committee, you will have a much clearer picture of the types of things you need to think about and place in your dissertation.

So, what are some of the resources you might seek out to help gain a better understanding of the dissertation process at your university? A few examples are listed below.

Resources from the University and/or Program

- Dissertation Guidebook
- Dissertation Template
- Dissertation Evaluation Rubric

Resources from Your Mentor and Committee

- Past dissertations of which she or he has participated, possibly including your committee members' dissertations.
- Names of others learners working with your mentor

Other Helpful Resources

- Publication Manual of the American Psychological Association (a.k.a. *APA Manual*)
- Other published dissertations (Check the UMI ProQuest database at your university library) on your topic area or that use your chosen methodology and/or analysis

Keep in mind that it is not just enough to find these resources. You need to seriously review them as well. You might even consider consulting with your mentor and committee to see what additional suggestions they have.

Organizing Your Resources (and thoughts!)

Something that you likely already learned from your experiences taking the Comprehensive or Qualifying Exam at your university is that you have many, many journal articles! For your dissertation, you probably can expect the number of peer-reviewed journal articles you have read and will use in your writing to double or triple. What are you going to do with all of these articles? How can you create order from the chaos of 100 to 200 articles that may be appropriate for your dissertation? I'll share some personal tricks that have worked for my mentees and me.

When I was working on my dissertation, I developed a system for categorizing and storing all of the articles I read. Because I completed my dissertation before the days when journals were largely available online, I would visit the library and make a photocopy of the peer-reviewed articles that may have a place in my dissertation. I would take them home, read them, and highlight those elements of the articles that had relevance to my dissertation. From there, I simply would spread out the articles on the floor into piles. I had one pile for articles that related to the particular methodology and sample that I was going to use. I had other piles related to the theory that served as the backbone of my research. Once I had completed an initial sort, I would take each pile of articles and sort them even further. For instance, I would sort the articles on methodology into smaller piles that reflected the sample, the instruments, the type of methodology, and the proposed data analysis. You can see where this is going. Once I had the articles sorted by topic and how they related to my dissertation, I would sort the mini piles according to which would be used first in the dissertation.

Thus, after this exercise (which was repeated several times over the course of writing my dissertation) I had all my articles sorted and in the order they would most likely be presented in the dissertation. As a last step in my organization of the literature, I took all of those articles and placed them into larger three ring binders so I could find any article quickly. Why was this so helpful? The activity of sorting actually was an exercise in thinking. In sorting the articles and making determinations concerning relevance, logic, and flow, I was engaged in very high level critical thinking skills. Another reason this was so helpful was that after the sorting was finished, I had a good idea of where any particular study fit into the dissertation.

With technology today, there are options for how you might organize your research (and hence your thoughts!). If you print your articles, three ring binders still may be the most appropriate method of organization. If, however, you prefer to store your articles in electronic format on your computer, consider sorting them into folders and subfolders on your hard drive. I have shared these sorting tricks with many mentees. Invariably, they later tell me that their thoughts became clearer and more organized and that writing the dissertation became much easier after doing this exercise.

So far, you have started the process of preparing yourself for success. Yet, how do you plan to maintain the drive to continue when you get to a difficult passage or a difficult concept or hit an expected bump in the road?

Maintaining the Drive

You have increased your resilience by preparing mentally for the road ahead. Additionally, you have worked to create an environment for yourself that supports your success. So, what can you do when you do encounter a bump in the road?

First, let me say that I have never encountered a dissertation (my own, my colleagues, or my mentees) that did not run into some bumps along the road. A dissertation is a work of independent research and as such is almost always unpredictable. Even with the best intentions, sometimes things happen that can discourage even the most passionate learner. Two things to remember about obstacles: (1) They happen with everyone! The world is not conspiring against you, and (2) those who complete their dissertation work through these challenges, remain positive, and have Ph.D. after their name! There is no way to foretell what challenges you will face that will test your beliefs in yourself, but there are some things that you can do to remain resilient, persistent, and ultimately successful.

Peer Support

Your family and friends will love and support you in your journey. However, unless they have gone through this journey too, they will not fully understand what you are experiencing. The only people who really "get it" and can empathize at the deepest level are those who are going through the process too. Your fellow graduate learners who are working on their dissertation can be an amazing source of strength for you. Seek them out, not only when things are challenging, but when things are going well too. All of us (myself included) need lots of support to accomplish a goal of this magnitude. You are not alone in your journey, and I can guarantee that your fellow learners will be grateful that you reached out to them. Regardless of how you specifically maintain your relationships, staying in touch with fellow learners is one of the best steps you can take to maintain your motivation and resilience.

Maintaining Your Writing Schedule

Remember that success can be measured in very small steps. You should be working on your dissertation everyday. Whether you write a single sentence or a whole section, you need to keep working daily. Contributing to your dissertation each day allows your mind to stay engaged with the topic. Similarly, by recognizing a small success each day, you continue to reinforce your positive behaviors. You never allow yourself to enter the emotional spiral of not working on your dissertation, which may cause you to become fearful and overwhelmed by what is ahead of you. This fear then reduces the likelihood that you will work on your dissertation the next day, which only increases your anxiety level, making it even more unlikely that you will work on your dissertation. The spiral of fear and anxiety caused by a lack of action is, in my experience, the most common reason why learners struggle to complete their dissertation.

Maintaining Quality

You want to produce a dissertation that is not only accepted by your committee, but one with which you will be proud. Maintaining the quality of the dissertation throughout the entire dissertation phase is paramount. There are several ways to establish and maintain high standards in your research and writing, some of which have been discussed already in other chapters regarding differing contexts.

Use Primary Sources

There is no greater red flag to mentors and committee members than seeing references from websites, popular press, and other secondary sources. Your dissertation reflects *your* analysis, synthesis, and evaluation of research. What mentors and committee members want to see is *your* evaluation of the research, not someone else's as is the case with secondary sources. Using primary, peer-reviewed sources in your dissertation will help to maintain a high level of quality.

Avoid Plagiarism

One thing that immediately discredits an author is plagiarism. If you copy, intentionally or unintentionally, another's work without giving proper credit, you have weakened the value of your work. Plagiarism has been discussed elsewhere in the book, so suffice it to say that you have to pay particular attention to this issue in your course work, comps exam, and your dissertation. There have been many published dissertations that in later years were found to contain significant plagiarized material. Regardless of the formal consequences, those authors' reputations will forever be tainted.

Pay Attention to the Evaluation Criteria

As I stated earlier when talking about resources that are available to you, the evaluation criteria or rubric used to assess your dissertation is common on university campuses. One thing that you can do to help you maintain the quality of your work is to print out the evaluation rubric and place it on the wall in your writing area. Refer to the rubric often as it is a guide for what to include in your dissertation. If for some reason your university or mentor does not use a rubric, create one yourself and share it with your mentor. Ask your mentor to review it with you so that you can come to a joint understanding of what is required.

Think, Write, Edit (T-W-E)

A simple mantra to help maintain quality and continuous progress while writing your dissertation is: **Think, Write, Edit.** When you are engaged in writing a particular section of your dissertation, first *think* about what needs to really be in there. Then *write* the text. Finally, return to the text you wrote and *edit* it for such things as spelling, grammar, structure, flow and transition, referencing, APA format, and accuracy.

Writing a dissertation is a different style of writing than most people are accustomed, and it often takes several drafts of a sentence, paragraph, section, chapter, even a proposal, to get it right. Everyone engaged in scientific writing does this; it is the nature of the game. Become comfortable with the pattern of Thinking, Writing, Editing and make it a healthy habit for your future writings as well.

Summary

Writing your dissertation will be one of the most challenging and rewarding opportunities in your life. There is no one "right" way to complete a dissertation, but there are many lessons to be learned from others who are either on the journey with you or have completed their dissertation. You can begin to prepare for your dissertation by preparing yourself for success. If you have made it to the dissertation phase, you have proved that you have the intelligence to complete a dissertation. Completing a dissertation, however, is much more than just a display of mental prowess. It is also about persistence, resilience, and a positive environment.

Take the time to mentally prepare for your dissertation. Remember, you are changing, so give yourself the time to prepare for that change. Take the time to gather and organize your resources. Talk with your mentor, your committee, and your fellow doctoral learners. You have many resources and support to help you produce a dissertation that is both high quality and finished!

Part VII

Wow, I Graduated!

Now What?

*You are rewarding a
teacher poorly if you remain
always a pupil.*

~Friedrich Nietzsche

I hope you never stop learning. As Tadashi Nakamura responded
to martial arts students regarding the completion of their training,
"There is no graduation date from the dojo." However, there comes a
time when the focus of self-learning, self-development, and personal
academic achievement needs to adjust to a new focus. Indeed, the
practice of knowledge formation and diffusion you conducted
through the dissertation should be at the heart of your post graduation
aspirations. Whether by publishing, teaching, mentoring, or some
other creative service, graduation means many things, not the least
of which is *paying it forward.*

The missing element, very likely, is a habit of mind: the constant, vigilant search for opportunities to make a difference.

~Dr. Peter Fiske
Author & Consultant
Career Development

Chapter

20

The Future Looks Bright!

Go confidently in the direction of your dreams!

~Henry David Thoreau

Earning a graduate degree, particularly a doctorate, can have a life changing effect. First, just consider what you accomplished by the journey itself. You have improved your critical thinking skills and capacity to evaluate the work of others. You have met different people and established new professional relationships. You have been a role model to everyone around you from your children to friends to co-workers - even your own parents. You even may have received a promotion at work in anticipation of the diploma. Beyond these achievements, earning your degree has given you a sense of empowerment and accomplishment probably exceeding anything else you have ever done. Now it is time to explore new opportunities and yes, give back for what you have been so fortunate to accomplish.

> *There is no more noble occupation in the world than to assist another human being – to help someone succeed.*
>
> *Alan Loy McGinnis*

So, what's next? What will you do with your new found time? What does the future hold? What will you do to make a difference? Let's take a look at a few specific endeavors that now may be viable options for you that may not have been in the past.

Teaching

I cannot think of a more rewarding endeavor than sharing my experiences with others. Even if teaching full-time is not one of your goals, maybe you should think about part-time teaching. If you crave the face-to-face energy, then consider a traditional school near your work or home. If you enjoyed your online learning experience, think about the multitude of opportunities you now have in the web-based world of higher education.

Many online programs and universities hire faculty without a Ph.D. to teach in their undergraduate programs. This is particularly true for adjunct faculty positions. However, it is very difficult to be hired into graduate programs without a doctorate. Obviously doctoral programs necessitate that faculty members possess a terminal degree whether in a traditional or online university. It's important to note, however, that earning your doctorate does not automatically open up once closed doors in the academic world. To land that full-time teaching position at a traditional school, you still will have to possess an impressive publishing history and more than likely have connections to the institution. While online universities appreciate a strong publishing record as well, they tend to be more focused on the scholar-practitioner model of doctoral education that honors publication practices yet also recognizes the potent value of practice expertise combined with scholarship. The University of Phoenix, Walden University, or Capella University, by illustration, might be more impressed with a substantial background and experience in the business world, human services field, or another discipline in which you are seeking to teach when combined with the demonstration of scholarship through the completion of your doctorate.

Another paradigm shift as a result of online higher education is the super dependence on adjunct or part-time faculty in the world of online higher education. According to Wickun and Stanley, adjunct instructors teach nearly 40% of all university courses in the United States. Although adjunct faculty members are very inexpensive compared to full-time faculty, the great news today with online programs is that adjuncts are not treated like second class educators. In a web-based course room setting, most students will not know whether the instructor is full-time (core faculty) or adjunct. Pay still is not what it could be at this stage in the evolution of adjunct compensation (generally between $1,000.00 and $4,000.00 per class); however, you will be treated with respect and your opinions and input will be valued. As a new Ph.D., keep in mind that you may have to "pay your dues" by starting off as an adjunct instructor while, at the same time, you will be building your resume should the day come when you are ready to make the leap to teaching full-time. As you are gaining experience on the instructor side of online education, you are also bringing keen insights to that endeavor that will enrich how you teach. You'll also be sharing your voice of experience as a graduate from an online program; such wisdom will be highly prized by the learners you teach.

Speaking Opportunities

While some of you, like me, frequently engaged in public speaking prior to earning your doctorate, many of you may not have had this wonderful experience. Equipped with the letters P H D after your name and original research from your dissertation, you may be very marketable as a public speaker.

Professional speaking can be rewarding on many levels. You will have opportunities to earn substantial income, travel to diverse and sometimes exotic locations throughout the country (or world), meet new people, learn how different organizations operate and behave, and most importantly, expand your professional reach. Clinical psychologist Jeff Zimmerman observed, "Public speaking is invigorating. It adds diversity to my practice and gives me a chance to apply my skills to a broader group of people than I can reach in my office."

As with any new or potentially challenging endeavor, you may need to establish yourself first before the money comes rolling your way. Don't be afraid in the beginning to accept non-paid or minimally paid speaking engagements. These opportunities will afford you time to build credibility, hone your presentation and speaking skills, and establish a demand for your services. Quite frequently, I have professional speakers, new and seasoned, offer to present at the FBI Academy without compensation. This serves three purposes for them. They get to give a little back to people protecting our nation, they get their face and product out in the public view, and they earn a nice addition to their resume, which will help them with future speaking endeavors.

There are various ways to get your name out on the lecture circuit. Local civic organizations always are looking for speakers. Consider offering to present to one or more of these groups. Be inclusive by expanding your reach to close to home non-profit organizations such as your child's Parent Teacher Organization. Remarkably, these speaking engagements sometimes generate other requests from parents who become part of your referral network. Consider talking with professionals who already are in the public speaking field. They can be powerful resources for advice and referral opportunities. To get your name "out there", do not be shy about networking and conversing with people as a way for others to see you have something of worth to offer their organization. Numerous public speaking associations exist to help in this endeavor such as Toastmasters and the National Speakers Association.

The most important thing to remember is to give clients something of value that they are not getting somewhere else. This book was written from this philosophy. After searching all the book stores and Internet for weeks and weeks, I found very little of substance that helped prospective and existing students truly navigate the world of online higher education. I saw a need and attempted to fill that need with this text. I suggest you do the same as you enter the wonderful world of professional speaking.

Consulting

According to Career Overview, the management consulting business alone employs over 300,000 people and represents a $30 billion industry. Whether part-time or full-time, consulting is a great way to earn an income, assist clients find new solutions to problems, deliver and manage projects, and share your expertise for the greater good.

Consulting opportunities run the gamut from someone who simply addresses a group of people in the organization in the role of a professional speaker all the way to being a quasi full-time member of the organization in the role of change manager, executive coach, information technology consultant, or a plethora of other roles. Consulting firms range from one person businesses to major operations like Booz, Allen, Hamilton or Accenture or McKinsey & Company.

Most top companies, as well as federal agencies, employ scores of consultants in one fashion or the other. While a great message and substantial experience may land you a consulting gig, having the letters P H D behind your name clearly may tilt the scale in your favor with regard to competition, financial compensation, and credibility. Most importantly, your doctoral journey honed your problem solving and critical thinking skills, which are precisely the key attributes needed to be a successful consultant.

Research

Certainly, one of the pillars of a doctoral education is research. The courses, comprehensive exam, and dissertation combine to produce a graduate who has demonstrated an ability to conduct original research. Many Ph.D.s carry these new skills into their existing work environment, or they may make a career change into the field of research. The opportunities are plentiful from the physical sciences, to social sciences, to medicine, or even engineering.

One word of advice – If you choose to begin a serious career in research, particularly in the university setting, you undoubtedly will need to understand funding and grant processes. Grants require biographical sketches of the primary researcher and research team. It is important for researchers to be well published in the research area as grant reviewers consider this information during the scoring process. A well developed publication list, including peer-reviewed and non peer-reviewed articles, attests to the researcher's capacity to successfully complete a project of value and thus strengthens the likelihood of obtaining funding.

Discovery of the unknown is at the heart of research; it is at the core of our humanity. For some new graduates, research will spark an interest and feeling of gratification unlike any other endeavor.

Publishing

The *publish or perish* paradigm in academe is very much alive and well, particularly within traditional, brick and mortar settings. This paradigm refers to the pressure exerted on faculty to conduct research and publish their findings to the greater community within their discipline. Types of publications vary from discipline to discipline, yet one thing is consistent. Universities want their professors to publish in scholarly venues.

Publishing also has financial implications to institutions of higher learning. Grants and other funding sources are a big deal in the world of higher education. Research and subsequent publishing contribute to the factors that bring in those dollars.

The *publish or perish* paradigm also the reflects the idea that universities will want to know what you have accomplished before they invest in you with regard to hiring, promotions, or even funding your next research endeavor. So, if you decide to head into the world of collegiate teaching and want to climb the ladder of instructor, assistant professor, associate professor, professor, earning tenure somewhere along the way, then prepare yourself for a life publishing. This is one of the reasons I am enamored with reputable online programs. They tend to focus on hiring and developing exceptional teachers as opposed to hiring and developing a faculty cadre who focuses more on publishing than on teaching students.

I do not want to play down the role of publishing. Publishing can be extremely rewarding on many levels. Some faculty members and researchers thrive in a publishing environment. As you will read in the next chapter, some graduates go on to publish in very significant ways and earn tenure rapidly, where others pace themselves more and focus on other aspects of academia. Academic publishing can bring welcome attention to you and your university by adding valuable research and insights to the body of knowledge in your field. Even non-scholarly publications, like this book, potentially offer positive visibility for authors and their institutions.

Mentoring

Possibly the greatest gift, the greatest contribution, you can offer is to help others along the path you chose. One of the key responsibilities of any leader is to create new leaders. This is true in higher education as well. Who better to encourage a passion for life-long learning than you?

Mentoring can be a formal endeavor. Capella University, for example, uses a formal mentoring process during both the comprehensive exam and dissertation phases. However, mentoring also may be exercised in a very informal manner. Almost daily, certainly two or three times a week, I get a phone call, personal visit, or email from someone thinking about pursuing a doctorate or from a current doctoral learner. The questions from potential students cover a broad range. What is a doctoral program really like? Is it similar to getting another master's degree? Which schools are best? Tell me about online learning. Tell me about accreditation. How much time will it require? Was it all worth it? Questions from current students also cover a wide range. "Doc, one instructor told me to do it this way, but another one said to do it that way?" "I'm desperately trying to come up with a dissertation topic – help!" These are just a few of the questions and conversations I have on a very frequent basis.

Even though I love talking about higher education and equally love fanning that fire in others, I really do not have time for many of these conversations. I put in very long hours with my full time career as well as adjunct teaching at Capella with all of those associated responsibilities. Not to mention, my favorite hobby in the world is spending time with my family. HOWEVER, I have a responsibility, a moral obligation if you will, to help others along. *All Ph.D.s do.* Let me close this chapter with my favorite poem. The author of this specific version is unknown, however, the original version of the poem was written by Will Allen Dromgoole, a prolific poet who lived 1860-1934.

Building Bridges for Tomorrow

An old man on a lonesome road,

came at evening gray and cold,

to a chasm deep and wide,

through which there flowed a sullen tide.

The old man crossed in the twilight dim;

The stream it held no fears for him.

But when he reached the other side,

he built a bridge to span the tide.

"Old man," said a fellow pilgrim near,

"why waste your time building here?

Your journey's o'er at the end of day;

You never again will pass this way.

You've crossed this chasm deep and wide;

Why build you this bridge at eventide?"

The builder lifted his old gray head.

"Good friend, on this path," he said,

"there follows after me today,

a lad who too must pass this way.

This chasm that's meant naught to me,

to that fair lad may a peril be.

He too must cross in the twilight dim;

Good friend, I build this bridge for him."

Chapter 21

Keeping It Real

Personal Thoughts from Online Graduates

Graduates of web-based programs are in the ideal position to provide an accurate evaluation of the relevance of their online learning experience with regard to their personal interests and career aspirations. Williford and Moden (1989) observed that graduates have a greater capacity to assess the true value and quality of their education relative to their post graduation experiences.

To this end and to provide a unique, personal touch to the conclusion of this book, I asked several alumni from regionally accredited and reputable online degree programs to candidly share their experience as a student, and most importantly, the impact their online degree has had for them post graduation. Enjoy!

Rodney (Rod) Hicks, Ph.D., R.N., FNP-CS
Capella University
Class of 2006

Professor

UMC Health System Endowed Chair for Patient Safety

Texas Tech University Health Sciences Center

School of Nursing

Lubbock, Texas 79430

Mentorship is the relationship formed from the wise experience and trust of counselors or guides with a lesser experienced person. This word is only three syllables in length, yet its influence lasts a lifetime. Since Greek times, society has come to value mentorship for it remains evident in the organizations in which we work, the sacred places we worship, and how we guide the young. In addition, I believe mentorship is needed during educational endeavors, during career planning, and throughout one's personal life. I would like to share how Capella University's mentorship has helped me in these three areas.

I had been advised by colleagues to obtain only a regionally accredited degree so the degree would be universally recognized. That bit of knowledge put me on the pursuit of an online program that was flexible enough to meet my employment responsibilities while affording me a quality education. My experiences of Capella's mentorship began from the first inquiry about the doctoral program in the School of Human Services. The Capella admission counselor, Ryan Gould, guided me through the degree plan, answered all my questions about the application process, and facilitated the transfer of knowledge about what online graduate education meant. He mentored me about the weekly exchange of assignments and thwarted any ability for me to be a procrastinator. Rather, I would be engaging in scholarly discussions from the beginning of each course until its end with no opportunity to fall behind. I later learned that this type of engagement is necessary for retention and learner success in the cyber world of higher education.

Through prior graduate studies, I was introduced to mentorship, though, as it turned out, it was only pseudo-mentorship given that those schools and faculty only gave lip service to guiding students. So, during the first quarter, I remained a little skeptical about the value of the online program format and mentorship at Capella. My *FirstCourse* instructor worked with me on the mechanics of APA and scholarly writing, laying the foundation of what would become the first of more than 100 published papers.

At the end of the first quarter, I traveled to Scottsdale, Arizona, to attend my first residential colloquia. During the week, it was clear this is where the rubber met the road, and mentorship was the key to success in obtaining a Ph.D. I developed a strong sense that Capella always would provide me, the learner, unrelenting support. It was also at this time that I met the residency director and key faculty from my school, further reinforcing that I would not be alone during my studies. Rather, I would trust these talented individuals to provide me the necessary guidance to complete my program. I also was fortunate that at that time, I was able to be assigned a program mentor, who remained at my side through graduation. At each residency, my mentor sat with me and my schedule to ensure that I received what I needed, when I needed it, all with an eye towards building the trust in the process to successfully complete the dissertation.

For the next several quarters, I made it a point to remain in contact with my cohort leaders and my mentor so that by the end of each quarter these inspiring individuals knew my interests and accomplishments. Their feedback served not only to reinforce my desire to graduate but also how each of the courses would ultimately support my planned study.

Two residencies and several quarters later, it was time for the comprehensive examination. I truly believe that during this process, I personally recognized my self-transformation from the doctoral student role to the new role that awaited me – a true scholar-practitioner fully grounded upon my personal ambition and hard work and through the mentorship Capella provided. My dissertation quickly followed, and I finally had the Ph.D. in hand ready to contribute to a better society.

My Capella mentorship experience also provided me with additional self-reflection in my own career. While it is widely recognized that the Ph.D. can open new doors, my new reflection taught me that just to pass through a new door is not enough. It was the values and beliefs accompanying me on the passage that served as the compass through my career journey. By virtue of Capella's mentorship following graduation, I learned that as I changed, the people I worked with probably were not likely to change in the same manner. I yearned for mentee/mentor opportunities.

About a year and half following graduation, I changed employers and went to a new setting with different challenges and opportunities. Currently, I am in my mid to upper career as a tenured professor and endowed chair (both within two years of graduating from Capella) with responsibilities to mentor those behind me, while building important relationships with those leading our organization. This is, after all, what professionals do with other professionals.

In one's personal life, at least for me, mentorship is as important as the other many roles. I believe that finding the balance between work and home is often difficult but not insurmountable. I look to people outside my profession and away from the workplace to help me juggle life demands and keep me humble and grounded. Several of these people have been at my side for many years. Today I welcome, rather than resist, opportunities to receive mentorship from those older as well as to provide mentorship to those younger than me.

Capella University's mastery of mentorship will continue to shape the future, not only in our country, but around the world. As a scholar-practitioner, I believe in the universality of mentorship and its influence on any professional or personal role and forever will be indebted to the quality of mentorship provided to me during my time with Capella.

Greg M. Vecchi, Ph.D.
Nova Southeastern University
Class of 2006

Chief
Behavioral Sciences Unit
FBI Academy
Quantico, Virginia 22135

I have been involved with online learning for many years both as a graduate student and adjunct professor. I began my doctoral work in Conflict Analysis and Resolution at Nova Southeastern University in Fort Lauderdale, Florida, in a traditional, residential program. However, after accepting a faculty position at the FBI Academy, I moved to an online format to complete my coursework. Make no mistake, the rigor and work requirements were the same online as they were I was working on my degree in-residence.

Online learning has pros and cons as does everything. The greatest advantage for me was the convenience and portability it offered. The asynchronous environment provided the ability to attend school anywhere at anytime and even allowed me to continue teaching when I was deployed to Baghdad, Iraq, in support of the FBI's counterterrorism mission. The biggest disadvantages of online learning are the lack of face-to-face interpersonal contact with the professor and other students and the heavy reliance on technology. Most students do very well in this environment, but some need more interpersonal contact with the instructor in order to grasp complicated concepts such as statistics. Procrastinators may find this environment too demanding as well.

The Ph.D. has opened many doors for me as well as expanded my reach and credibility in my current career. I find myself being invited to professional conferences with increasing frequency. I now consult more than ever within and outside the FBI and will continue to do so in my post FBI life. I also serve as an adjunct instructor and member of numerous dissertation committees, which would not have been possible without the doctorate.

I know my professional future is bright and that largely is a result of earning the Ph.D. I have absolutely no regrets about earning my doctorate in the online setting. My degree is just as respected as if I completed all the material face-to-face. Online learning has its drawbacks as does traditional learning settings, but overall I would highly recommend it to the vast majority of learners considering graduate school.

Amy Williamson, M.S.
Florida State University
Class of 2006

Librarian

San Antonio Public Library System

The greatest features of my online education were flexibility and access to specialized learning. I wanted to earn a degree that local, brick and mortar universities did not offer. The availability of an online graduate degree program made all the difference to me. If the online education option had not been open, I would not have been able to pursue a degree in my chosen field. That flexibility and access became even more important toward the end of my studies when my child was born during the second week of my last semester. I had a short paper due seven days after his birth. This event would have caused a major disruption in a traditional school structure, but I was able to continue with only minor turbulence as I was excused from my virtual classes while in the hospital. The bottom line is that earning a Master's degree in Library Science simply would have been out of my reach without the online platform.

There is certainly something to be said for face-to-face classroom interaction, and that exchange is difficult to duplicate in an online setting. I did miss the more personal interaction of a physical learning environment. I also had to bring a high degree of self-motivation and discipline to my program that may not have been quite as needed in a traditional program.

My overall experience with online learning was very positive, and I would recommend it to most students, particularly adult learners with full-time careers. I truly benefited from a rigorous program and a faculty who cared about the quality and integrity of the program and about my success. I feel confident that my professional skills absolutely are equivalent to those of librarians who attended face-to-face classes.

Benjamin Davis, Ph.D., D.Min.
Northcentral University
Class of 2005

When Jeff invited me to talk about my experience with online learning at Northcentral University (NCU), I jumped at the opportunity. The experience has had a profound impact on my life, and the chance to share this with others was too good to pass up. I found NCU because a student shared her excitement with me, and I am honored and delighted to share my excitement and satisfaction with others.

My experience with NCU was fantastic. The school was exceedingly responsive and caring. From pre-enrollment to course work to commencement and beyond, every question I have had has been quickly answered, and everyone has gone out of their way to make my experience a good one. I also found the mentors (faculty) to be outstanding. To a person, they focused on my work and offered sound advice and quick feedback. I was able to direct my efforts towards my own interests, which made my studies have immediate relevance in my profession as well as in the classroom.

If there are three words that reflect my educational experience, they are flexibility, rigor, and responsiveness. One of the key factors that attracted me to NCU was the flexibility to manage my own process. I wanted a program that would allow me to move at my own pace and that would not have artificial impediments to my progress. Northcentral provided that every step of the way.

The program was flexible, but flexible does not mean easy. My program clearly was rigorous, and my mentors were wonderful. I learned much, and I was pleased with how well one course fit with the next. A bane of traditional programs is slow feedback from faculty and inattentive administrative staff. That was far from the case for me. Feedback was rapid and substantive, and my issues always were addressed quickly and thoroughly.

Like most adult learners, I had a busy schedule. Most traditional and many online programs have a very structured format throughout each course. One of the unique aspects that made Northcentral great was that I was able to match my pace through the courses to the time I had available. When my work load was relatively light, I moved rapidly. When I was swamped, I took the full time available for the course. The mentors respected my needs and were supportive whichever approach I took.

The dissertation is often a stumbling block for doctoral students. The world is filled with ABDs (All But Dissertation), but that generally is not the case for Northcentral students. The dissertation process is structured such that you would have to work at *not* finishing on time. It would be possible not to finish, but the way the process is structured, you won't want to.

Concerns about the acceptance of a degree earned through an online program are legitimate, and there remains some bias even today. Higher education can be very hide-bound, and change comes slowly. Those with a few years on them likely can remember the great concern when degrees in African-American Studies, Women's Studies, and General Studies were first introduced in the 1960s and 70s. Less than a century before that, educators were slow to allow degrees in engineering to be taught along side of *real* college courses. Today there is no question about these fields. The same is rapidly becoming true for online education. With technology as pervasive as it has become in business, with educational technology having become so robust, and with every major university offering courses and degrees in an online modality, it is only a matter of time before there will be neither question nor concern.

Some of the concerns about the value and validity of an online degree should be assuaged by accreditation. NCU is accredited by the same agency (the Higher Learning Commission of the North Central Association) that accredits the University of Michigan, Notre Dame, and Minnesota. The business programs have ACBSP accreditation, too. Northcentral is respected in academe as well. My tuition was paid by another university, and I am convinced that I received a promotion there and a position at another university as a direct result of my work at NCU.

My friends sometimes tell me that I sound like a commercial for online learning and particularly, Northcentral University. I suppose I am, but I really like to share my educational experiences. The flexibility and rigor of my program and the level of service NCU personally provided really won me over and has served me exceptionally well both personally and professionally.

Charles Tiffin, Ph.D.
The Union Institute and University
Class of 1998

Retired Police Major

Fulbright Fellow

Senior Core Faculty

Former Provost and Vice President of Academic Affairs

Capella University

Minneapolis, Minnesota 55402

From my earliest childhood memories, I was inquisitive and interested in learning more about the world, which must have sparked my interest in lifelong learning. During my journey, I have realized that education not only served as a backdrop to my life, but actually enabled my success. This vignette provides an overview of that journey.

As a teen, I joined the army as a military police officer. I served with the 118th MP Company (Airborne) at Ft. Bragg. I immediately began to think about college and explored several of the local programs. When I left the military, I joined what was, at that time, the country's largest consolidated public safety department. I was dually trained in police and fire responsibilities and thoroughly loved the role of helping my community. I began classes almost immediately at my local community college where I completed an associate's degree in police science. Thereafter, I completed another associate's degree in fire technology. I discovered early that I relished the opportunity to learn and apply my newfound knowledge in the application of my chosen profession. My earliest lesson was time management, and the appreciation that time must be allocated and scheduled for school work.

Once I finished my work at the community college, I attended Guilford College and earned a bachelor's in criminal justice and policy studies. I stuck with my time management strategy and again was able to carve out time for classes, studies and papers. I continued to enjoy learning and education while also finding it increasingly more difficult to find the time to successfully navigate competing demands. The daily two hour school commute was much more of a grind than I had expected, and there were times when I thought about dropping out. Yet, I persevered and earned my bachelor's degree.

I soon realized that I wanted to attend graduate school, but I loathed any thought of commuting. Fortunately, I had the opportunity to study in my home town and take courses that satisfied my intellectual curiosity from across the graduate schools at Duke University. Although my policing career often conflicted with my class times, I was able to persevere and eventually earn my master's degree in liberal studies.

Finally, as the lifelong learner that I had become, it was time to take the next step – the terminal degree. I explored various options and realized my career would not allow for me to take the type of educational leave necessary to complete a doctoral in-residence program. So, I opted for a different approach to obtain my degree and enrolled at The Union Institute (now The Union Institute and University). This program was an interdisciplinary program that allowed me to explore my varied interests in criminal justice, the intersection of race and gender, and organizational development. This learning pedagogy, as a virtual university, worked brilliantly vis-à-vis my duties as a police commander. I found that the forward-looking nature of my doctoral courses, seminars, workshops and residencies allowed me to continue with my policing career. I absolutely know that if I had opted for a brick and mortar program I would have had to put policing aside and certainly would not have risen to the executive ranks before retirement.

For me, earning my Ph.D. was life changing and has created incredible opportunities. One example is the wonderful opportunity of being associated with Capella University as we serve to provide educational opportunities to those in public safety. Our cities, towns, states, and country need thoughtful, insightful, and critically thinking leaders for the challenges ahead. For me, there is no better preparation for these challenges than furthering one's formal education! It has changed my life and can change yours as well!

Sources

Airaksinen, T. (1988). An analysis of coercion. *Journal of Peace Research, 25*(3), 213-227. Retrieved January 26, 2008, from http://jpr.sagepub.com/cgi/content/abstract/25/3/213

Al-Awqati, Q. (2007). Plagiarism. *Kidney International, 71*(2), 91-92.

American Psychological Association. (2001). *Publication manual of the American Psychological Association* (5th ed.). Washington, DC: Author.

Anderson, L., & Krathwohl, D. (Eds.). (2001). *A taxonomy for learning, teaching, and assessing: A revision of Bloom's Taxonomy of educational objectives.* New York: Longman.

Backlar, P. (1998). Anticipatory planning for research participants with psychotic disorders like schizophrenia. *Psychology, Public Policy, and Law, 4*(3), 829-853.

Babb, D., & Mirabella, J. (2007). *Make money teaching online: How to land your first academic job, build credibility, and earn a six-figure salary.* Hoboken, NJ: John Wiley & Sons, Inc.

Bartz, W. R. (2002, Sep/Oct). Teaching skepticism via the CRITIC acronym and the Skeptical Inquirer [Electronic version]. *The Skeptical Inquirer, 30,* 59–60.

Beecher, H. (1966). Ethics and clinical research. *New England Journal of Medicine, 274,* 1354-1360.

Bélanger, C. (2006). *How to recognize scholarly sources.* Retrieved February 9, 2008, from http://faculty.marianopolis.edu/c.belanger/quebechistory/Howtorecognizeascholarlysource.html

Berg, J. (1996). Legal and ethical complexities of consent with cognitively impaired research subjects: Proposed guidelines. *Journal of Law, Medicine & Ethics, 24,* 18-35.

Blanchard, K. (1985). *Leadership and the one minute manager.* New York: William Morrow and Company.

Bloom, B. (Ed.) (1956). *Taxonomy of educational objectives: The classification of educational goals, by a committee of college and university examiners: Handbook I.* New York: Longmans, Green.

Boote, D., & Beile, P. (2005). *Scholars before researchers: On the centrality of the dissertation literature review in research preparation, 34*(6), 3-15.

Bradshaw, M., & Lowenstein, A. (2007). *Innovative teaching strategies in nursing and related health professions* (4th ed.). Sudbury, MA: Jones and Bartlett.

Brown, R. (2007). *The secret to online success at Axia College and the University of Phoenix: The definitive guide to making As online.* Short and Sweet Books.

Bruner, J. (1966). *Toward a theory of instruction.* Cambridge, MA: Belkapp Press.

Capella University. *Academic honesty - policy statement.* Retrieved January 28, 2008, from Faculty iGuide at https://portal.capella.edu

Capella University. *Use of human participants/subjects in research – policy statement.* Retrieved February 14, 2008, from Faculty iGuide at https://portal.capella.edu

Career Overview. *Consulting Career, Job, and Training Information* Retrieved March 5, 2008, from http://www.careeroverview.com/consulting-careers.html

Charleston Southern University. *Plagiarism tutorial.* Retrieved January 21, 2008, from http://www.csuniv.edu/library/ Plagiarism/ quote.htm

Christ, F., & Ganey, L. (2003). *100 things every online student ought to know.* Williamsville, NY: Cambridge Stratford LTD.

Churchill, W. Quote retrieved from http://www.thinkexist.com

Clark, C., & Ramsey, R. Teaching and learning at a distance. In *Teaching in Nursing: A guide for faculty* (2nd Ed.). St. Louis, MI: Elsevier Saunders.

Code of Federal Regulations. (1991). Federal policy for the protection of human subjects. *Federal Register, 56*, 28012-28018.

Coolidge, C. Quote retrieved from http://www.thinkexist.com

Covey, S. (1998). *The 7 habits of highly effective teens.* New York: Simon & Schuster, Inc.

Cover, S. R. (1988). *The 7 habits of highly effective people. Powerful lessons in personal change.* New York: Simon & Schuster.

Sources

Creswell, J. (2003). *Research design: Qualitative, quantitative, and mixed methods approaches* (2nd ed.). Thousand Oaks, CA: Sage.

Department of Health, Education, and Welfare. (1979). *The Belmont report: Ethical principles and guidelines for the protection of human subjects of research.* Retrieved January 14, 2008, from http://www.hhs.gov/ohrp/humansubjects/guidance/Belmont/htm

Disney, W. Quote retrieved from http://www.thinkexist.com

Distance Education and Training Council. (2007). *2007 distance education survey.* Retrieved January 30, 2008, from http://www.detc.org/downloads/2007DESurvey.pdf

Distance Education and Training Council. (2010). DETC news. Retrieved June 1, 1010, from *http://www.detc.org/downloads/publications/DETC%20News%20-%20 Fall%202009.pdf*

Eaton, J. (1996). *An overview of U.S. accreditation.* Retrieved February 5, 2008, from http://www.chea.org/pdf/ overview_ S_accred_8-03.pdf

Elliot, T. S. (1963). Little gidding (last stanza). *Collected Poems, 1909 - 1962* (The Centenary Edition.). Orlando, FL: Harcourt Brace and Company.

Facione, P. (1990). *Critical thinking: A statement of expert consensus for purposes of educational assessment and instruction. The Delphi Report.* Newark, DE: American Philosophical Association. Retrieved January 12, 2008, from http://www.insightassessment.com/ pdf_files/DEXadobe.PDF

Festinger, L., & Carlsmith, J.M. (1959). Cognitive consequences of forced compliance. *Journal of Abnormal and Social Psychology, 58,* 203-210.

Fiske, P. (2006). *Opportunities.* Retrieved February 24, 2008, from http://sciencecareers.sciencemag.org/career_development/previous_issues/articles/2006_09_08/opportunities/(parent)/68

Gallagher, J., Dobrosielski-Vergona, K., Wingard, R., & Williams, T. (2005). Web-based vs. traditional classroom instruction in gerontology: A pilot study. *Journal of Dental Hygiene, 79*(3), 1-10.

Gassaway, L. (2003). *When U.S. works pass into the public domain.* Retrieved February 2, 2008, from http://www.unc.edu/~unclng/public-d.htm

Gergen, D. (2009). Address at Capella University Colloquium. Retrieved June 1, 2010, from http://www.capella.edu/publicservice/transcripts/transcript_gergen.html

Gibbon, E. (1776). *Decline and Fall of the Roman Empire, Chap. lxviii.* As cited on Bartleby.com retrieved January 02, 2008, from http://www.bartleby.com/100/290.html

Gilbert, S. (2001). *How to be a successful online student.* New York: McGraw-Hill.

Gibran, K. (1986). *The voice of the master* (A. R. Ferris, Trans.). New York: Carol Publishing Group. (Original work published 1958).

Glatthorn, A. (1998). *Writing the winning dissertation: A step by step guide.* Thousand Oaks, CA: Corwin Press, Inc.

Glicken, M. (2003). *Social research: A simple guide.* Boston, MA: Pearson Education.

Gubernick, L., & Ebeling, A. (1997). I got my degree through E-mail. *Forbes,* 159, 84-92.

Heeger, G. In Gilbert, S. (2001). *How to be a successful online student* (p. x). New York: McGraw-Hill.

Herbert, F. Quote retrieved from http://www.thinkexist.com

Huitt, W. (2004). Bloom et al.'s taxonomy of the cognitive domain. *Educational Psychology Interactive.* Valdosta, GA: Valdosta State University. Retrieved February 21, 2008, from http://chiron.valdosta.edu/whuitt/col/cogsys/ bloom.html

Humphreys, L. (1975). *Tearoom trade.* Chicago: Aldine. James, H. (1955). *Selected letters: Edited by Leon Edel.* New York: Farrar, Straus, and Cudsky.

James, K. (2005). News Release. *OPM Director Kay Coles James Announces Stricter Guidelines Regarding Diploma Mills.* Retrieved March 17, 2008, from http://www.opm.gov/news/opm-director-kay-coles-james-announces-stricter-guidelines-regarding-diploma-mills,771.aspx

Kalmbach, M.A., & Lyons, P.M. (2003). Special report: Ethical and legal standards for research in prisons. *Behavioral Sciences and the Law, 21*, 671-686.

Sources

Kendall, J., & Pogue, K. (2006). Survey of alumni from distance degree and campus-based baccalaureate programs. *Quarterly Review of Distance Education, 7*(2), 155-165.

Krathwohl, D. (2002). A revision of Bloom's taxonomy: An overview. *Theory into Practice, 41*(4), 212-218.

Latane, B., & Darley, J.M. (1968). Group inhibition of bystander intervention in emergencies. *Journal of Personality and Social Psychology, 10*, 215-221.

Marsh, H. (2001). Effects of grading leniency and low workload on students' evaluations of teaching. *Journal of Educational Psychology, 92*(1), 202-229.

McCabe, D. Research on academic integrity. *The Center for Academic Integrity*. Retrieved January 28, 2008, from, http://www.northwestern.edu/uacc/cai/ research/highlights.html

McGinnis, A. Quote retrieved from http://www.thinkexist.com.

Meyer, K. (2006). When topics are controversial: Is it better to discuss them face-to-face or online? *Innovative Higher Education, 31*(3), 175-186.

Milgram, S. (1963). Behavioral study of Obedience. *Journal of Abnormal and Social Psychology, 67*, 371–378.

Moulton, P., & Moulton, M. (2006). *Using Brooks/Cole's online resources effectively: A primer for instructors*. Belmont, CA: Thomson.

Nakamura, T. (1992). *One day-one lifetime*. New York: World Seido Karate Organization.

Newsome, C. (1997). *A Teacher's Guide to Fair Use and Copyright*. Retrieved February 2, 2008, from http://home.earthlink.net/~cnew/ research.htm

Nietzsche, F. Quote retrieved from http://www.thinkexist.com

Northrup, P. (2002). Online learners' preferences for interaction. *The Quarterly Review of Distance Education, 3*(2), 219–226.

O'Neill, T., & Novak, W. (1987). *Man of the house: The life and political memoirs of Speaker Tim O'Neill*. New York: Random House.

Online Colleges and Degrees. *Choosing an online college: Ten mistakes to avoid.* Retrieved February 1, 2008, from http://www.online-colleges-and-degrees.com/ choosing_ an_ online_college.htm. List used with permission.

Paiget, J. Quote retrieved from http://www.thinkexist.com

Patrick, P. (2007). *Doctoral Colloquia Faculty Handbook 2007-2008* Retrieved February 16, 2008, from Faculty iGuide – Residency Colloquium.

Pawlenty, T. *Address at Capella University.* Retrieved May 1, 2010, from http://www.capella.edu/PublicService/leading-the-way.asp

Phillips, V. (2000). *Are online degrees really as good as their campus counterparts?* Retrieved February 25, 2008, from https://www. geteducated.com

Powell, C. (2009). *Address at Capella University colloquium.* Retrieved May 19, 2010, from http://www.capella.edu/video/transcripts/powell_ transcript_1.html

Prochaska, J. O., & DiClemente, C. C. (1983). Stages and processes of self-change of smoking: Toward an integrative model of change. *Journal of Consulting and Clinical Psychology, 51,* 390-395.

Rohai, A. (2002). Building sense of community at a distance. *International Review of Research in Open and Distance Learning, 3(*1), 1-16.

Roig, M. *Avoiding plagiarism, self-plagiarism, and other questionable writing practices: A guide to ethical writing.* Retrieved March 17, 2008, from http://facpub.stjohns.edu/~roigm/plagiarism/.html

Sloan Consortium. (2006). *Making the grade: Online education in the United States, 2006.* Retrieved February 22, 2008, from http://www.sloan-c.org/ publications/survey/survey 06. asp

Sloan Consortium. (2007). *Online Nation: Five years of growth in online Learning.* Retrieved January 22, 2008, from http://www.sloan-c.org/ publications/survey/index.asp

Standler, R. (2000). *Plagiarism in colleges in USA.* Retrieved January 24, 2008, from http://www.rbs2.com/plag.htm

Sources

Thomas, S., & Quinn, S. (1991). The Tuskegee Syphilis Study, 1932 to 1972: Implications for HIV education and AIDS risk education programs in the black community. *American Journal of Public Health, 81*(11), 1498-1595.

Thompson, C. (2006). Unintended lessons: Plagiarism and university. *Teachers College Record, 108*(12), 2439-2449.

Tinto, V. (1993). *Leaving college: Rethinking the causes and cures of student attrition* (2nd ed.). Chicago: University of Chicago Press.

Sun Tzu. In Giles, L. (1988). *Sun Tzu on the art of war.* Graham Brash, Ltd.

United States Copyright Office. *Fair use.* Retrieved January 28, 2008, from http://www.copyright.gov/fls/fl102.html

University of Maryland University College. *History and vision.* Retrieved January 29, 2008, from http://www.umuc.edu/gen/about.shtml

University of Phoenix. *Fact Book 2007.* Retrieved January 24, 2008, from https://www.Phoenix.edu

Vasarhelyi, M., & Graham L. (1997, Aug.). Cybersmart: Education and the Internet. *Management Accounting,* 32-36.

Verrill, S. (2010). *Review comments of a comprehensive exam.* Capella University.

Walden University. *About us.* Retrieved January 28, 2008, from http://www.waldenu.edu/c/About/About.htm

Wells, O. Quote retrieved from http://www.thinkexist.com

Wehlage, G., Rutter, R., & Smith, G. (1989). *Reducing the risk: Schools as communities of support.* New York: The Falmer Press.

Wickun, R., & Stanley, W. *The role of adjunct faculty in higher education.* Retrieved March 6, 2008, from http://mtprof.msun.edu/Win2000/Wickun.html

Williford, A., & Moden, G. (1989). *Using alumni outcomes research in academic planning.* Paper presented at the annual forum of the Association for Institutional Research, Baltimore, MD.

Willis, B. In Gilbert, S. (2001). *How to be a successful online student* (p. 115). New York: McGraw-Hill.

World Medical Association (1964). *Declaration of Helsinki: Ethical Principles for Medical Research Involving Human Subjects.* Retrieved February 16, 2008, from http://www.wma.net/e/policy/ pdf/17c.pdf

Yale College. *Common knowledge.* Retrieved January 23, 2008, from http://www.yale.edu/bass/writing/sources/ plagiarism/common.html

Yeats, W. Quote retrieved from http://www.thinkexist.com/

Young, S., & Shaw, D. (1999). Profiles of effective college and university teachers. *The Journal of Higher Education, 70*(6), 670-686.

Zimmerman, J. (2005). As cited in *Professionally speaking: Tapping into the lecture circuit.* Retrieved February 26, 2008, from http://www. apapractice.org/apo/insider/practice/ marketing/lecture.html#

Index

Index